CONQUERING THE POWERS OF DARKNESS THROUGH FAITH

HAMENA JAPHET KOKOTE

COPYRIGHT

Copyright© Hamena .J. Kokote 2017

This book is sold subject to the condition that it shall not, by way of trade or otherwise, be lent, resold, hired out, or otherwise circulated without the publisher's prior consent in any form of binding or cover other than that in which it is published and without similar condition including this condition, being imposed on the subsequent purchaser

For enquiries and trade order contact :

HAMENA .J. KOKOTE

Email :hkokote@gmail.com

Phone : +254711981069

+254773082616

DEDICATION

For my wife, Loyce

CONTENTS

PREFACE

I started writing this testimonial book since 2009. I have written it out of God's love and compassion for all the lost sheep of God with much agony for those on the dark side of the world -the devil's agents. John 10:28 says " ***All those who are mine, I give them eternal life and they will not get lost. No one can be able to snatch them from my hands***"

Jesus Christ of Nazareth is the true answer to all people's problems on earth. Dear reader, you might be reading this testimony while you are bound by the devil. You might be a cigarette smoker, a drunkard, an adulterer, a hater, quarrelsome, sick, demon possessed or else, you have not yet let Jesus save your life. Jesus is calling you right now to heal you from all infirmities that you are encountering – Matt 11:28. All that is written in this book is true life experience. All the events written in this book are true except for some of the names of people and organizations which are just fabrications. This testimony has been written without any prejudice whatsoever. No one's church neither any other's religions that are noted in this book.

ACKNOWLEDGMENTS

I give all the glory to **God** for His divine protection, power and will. It is only the grace of **God** that had made me to write this book. I give much thanks to my wife **Loyce** and sister **Eunia Jilloh** for their accompaniment all along as we struggled in prayers and conquered all the powers of darkness through faith in **Jesus Christ**.

I also wish to acknowledge friends and relatives who took their time and resources to support the finishing of this booklet – **Conquering The Powers of Darkness Through Faith**.

Much thanks to **Joseph Nchore** of Mt. Pisgah Cyber-café –Likoni and **Tom Ocharo** of **Hatua Likoni** for dedicating their time in arranging and editing this book.

God bless you all.

CHAPTER 1

<u>ZUWENA-THE EVIL CHILD</u>

"Finally my brethren, be strong in the Lord, and in the power of His might! Put on the whole armor of God that ye may be able to stand against the wiles of the devil. For we wrestle not against flesh and blood, but against the rulers of darkness of this world, against spiritual wickedness in high places."
"Ephesians 6:10-18"

"2 Corinthians 10:3-6"

It was very early in the morning and my wife had already gone out for work. I had nowhere to go as our job was halt for some period of time and therefore, I just remained in bed. While I lay there, I started hearing some weird events going on outside the house and within the whole area. There happened to be a small kid (Zuwena) not her real name- within the average of twelve years whom seemed to be very much upset about me. She went everywhere raising her voice complaining all about me. I perceived that many people were gathering around her asking a lot of questions as she went on saying,

"Why does this old man Kokote, like polluting the air and sleeping? He has no job and also no children!"

As I learnt later, polluting the air to them meant praying or worshipping. Normally, whenever I missed somewhere to go or something to do, I had the habit of reading my bible, praying or worshipping and then sleeping. As I woke up, with nothing to do that morning, I found myself repeating the same thing. **"Well"** I thought,

"I don't have a stable job and that's true, children are from God and esteem and wealth come from God Proverbs 8:18-21. Then why should this be someone else's concern? Why shouldn't this kid learn manners? And why can't she come and face me directly and let the cat out of the bag?"

I later learnt that those things were happening spiritually and while I was fully awake. By then I was a born again Christian and I knew that I should stand firm in the Lord Jesus Christ so that I could be vindicated by Him. There is a verse that always strengthens and keeps me on moving that says,

"Save the ones taken to be killed; release the ones

who are ready to be slaughtered, if you say we did not know this then he who tries the heart doesn't he know? He who protects your soul, doesn't he understand? Then isn't He going to pay everyone according to his work?" Proverbs 24:11-12.

That spiritual battle continued up to the next day which was on a Sunday. I was in Malindi- Kenya by then. I used to fellowship at Good News church in the town centre under pastor Malibe (not his real name). I got ready and went to church for the Sunday service. As it was my usual habit, I sat on a bench near the back row of the church; where the pastor and the deacons of that church used to sit. The service went on as usual, but I could not help over hearing those weird events going on, in the spiritual realm which I alone was witnessing. I heard the pastor talking to one of the deacons; *"You see? Kokote is one of the people whom have held on to their salvation and has not yet back slidden: Now he is in the center of a spiritual warfare and he doesn't know about it."*

The deacon answered; *"I gave an order that no one should tell him of what is going on within his life because if they do so, they will be the first to pity him."*

This, I heard and perceived spiritually and I knew that I couldn't ask them of what they meant with those statements. So I remained silent and followed the service. The following day which was on a Monday, my wife was called by Sister Eunia to go to Mombasa to help her with some business. Sister Eunia is a born again Christian and the land lady of the house we were living in. I was left once more all alone in our rented house and so the devil was out to torment me harder. Zuwena came again to torment me, this time more furiously than before. She complained too much about me as I started seeing people in the spiritual world getting angry and furious with me, throwing dirty words at me. They were all on the dark side of the world, saying; ***"You fool! You are needed to be killed."***

"You shall be burned under a vehicle tyre." Another retorted.

The atmosphere was so tense for me, I had no knowledge that such forces could be rebuked and moved by the mighty name of Jesus Christ. I came to know that, Zuwena was continuously communicating to her superiors about all the activities I was undertaking at every given moment.

I could hear statements like;
"What is he   doing now?"

And she would answer, "He is taking a shower."

"And now, what's going on with him?"

"He is eating." "And now."

"He is sitting on his bed."

"He is polluting the air." (Meaning that I was praying).

The word of God says; "submit yourselves therefore to God, resist the devil and he will flee from you." James 4:7

If you are born again it's alright, but if not my dear brethren and you are in the center of such a spiritual warfare, press on forcefully to give your life to Jesus Christ. If you see there isn't a strong born again person to pray with you the prayer of repentance, you can pray this prayer by faith right now from wherever you are; *"My dear Lord Jesus Christ I am a sinner and I know this. Forgive me of all the sins and transgressions that I have committed against you. Erase my name from the book of death and write it in the book of life. Sanctify me with your precious blood. I am now born*

again in the mighty name of Jesus. "Amen!

You are now born again in Christ Jesus if you have prayed this prayer of repentance. What remains is only sanctification and prayers. Jesus has given us power and authority to tread upon serpents and cast out demons and heal the sick-Mark 16:15-18. One can win such a battle by the power and name of Jesus Christ. The word of God says;

"If ye abide in me, and my words abide in you, ye shall ask what ye will and it shall be done unto you." John 15:7.

As the fight went on, Zuwena got more furious as I heard a well Known young man and neighbor by the name (Nyundo) not his real name shouting, ***"It seems that things have become worse, why should Kokote be the one at the center of complaints always? Its time he is sent to the headman!"***

Inwardly, I squirmed and struggled so much. The situation was becoming serious and scary as I heard and witnessed those scenarios unfolding. That night,I took my supper, worshipped and prayed as was my usual habit before retiring to bed as this helped me relax and get some sleep easily. It was around 9:00 pm as I laid on my bed, I heard a meeting going on, and I was the main agenda in

that meeting. The headman, who was the chairman of that meeting/congregation, started asking questions; ***"Why is Zuwena and majority of the people complaining so much about Kokote? Why?"***A man rose up among that congregation and answered; ***"well, the kid seems to be affected and confused by Kokote's prayers. You know he is a mature born again Christian."***

A woman also stood up and said;

"Kokote is only being tormented for nothing. He is a born again Christian and very polite. He is a good person."The headman said; **"why do you answer on his behalf? Why can't he be brought here for judgment? Let him explain everything on his own."**

I almost froze as I pondered, **"Where is this place? And who are these people?"**That meeting ended at 11:00pm as sleep finally overtook me. Those weird meetings were conducted mostly during the night hours. During the day, I could hear people mainly from the dark spiritual world walking around cursing me and planning a lot of bad plans on how to eliminate me.

The next meeting started at seven pm the following night.

I usually went to bed at around 8:00 pm after worshipping and praying. I just laid there on bed as I perceived of the ongoing meeting. It was in my own knowledge that those meetings were conducted by people and demons. The headman, who always took the position of the chairman, was on the platform in front of that congregation. Apart from the others, the headman and a few of the chosen near him were Rastafarians (whom I perceived to be demons).

The rest I perceived to be mainly sorcerers, native doctors and the less active devil worshippers. Bhang was smoked and other drugs taken as a rule and that whole congregation was high on it. Bongo, reggae, local-Giriama and gospel music could be heard loud and clear from the stage.

I wondered as to why and how the devil could be able to play some gospel music from his pulpit and sometimes from people thought to be faithful and Godly people. The chairman could take the accent of a Kikuyu and at other times take the accent of a pure Giriama and a great native doctor at that. Most of the time, he talked via some amplified speakers/voice. His voice was very loud that if you gave your ears to it always, you could develop some stomach ulcers. He went on feeding his weird congregation with that weird music. At a certain point, the agenda of that meeting changed and I now became the center of concentration. The chairman whom had a loud and groggy voice started addressing that congregation and drew them to attention by saying;

"You see, Kokote is a total fool; he has no job, no children and even his wife is a devil worshipper and he doesn't know about it. When he sleeps with her, he does it with a snake and he doesn't recognize it. He likes polluting the air and sleeping. Today we shall bring him here so that he can explain himself on all these complaints."

Dear reader, although I am a very true and serious born again Christian, when I heard that statement, I shrunk under the bed covers. It was around 11:00pm and the situation had become more than worse for me and I said, **"Jesus- my master, whether these are demons or devil worshippers, I don't need them. I don't want to get anywhere near such a weird congregation and so I rebuke them in the mighty name of Jesus.**

CHAPTER 2

<u>**BREAKING SATAN'S STRONG HOLD**</u>

I couldn't cope to sleep all alone in the house as the situation had become too much provoking for me to withstand. I shot up from the bed, took the padlocks, locked the door from outside and at once, I rushed to my sister's house – Annie, almost four hundred meters away.

On my way, I only met a few people as most of them had already retired to bed. As I walked on, I could not help over hearing what was going on in that meeting. I was sweating and shivering as I thought;

"Hush! I am the most wanted."

I arrived at my sister's house, knocked at the door and as she opened, I told her that I was not feeling well and needed a place to sleep. She told me to join her sons in their bed. I laid there but before I slept, I asked her; *"Do you hear that meeting that is going on?"*

"Yes, it's a burial ceremony". She answered.

"It's alright then."

I said as I lay to sleep. I could not get to sleep so much easily as the atmosphere became very harsh.

As I lay there, I heard their headman commanding;

"I right now want two people to go straight to Kokote's house get him whether he likes it or not. Tie his hands and feet then bring him here. We want to hear everything straight from his mouth."

All this dear reader was coming to me expressly. Whether it was far or near, I could not help off hearing. Two people had shot off to where I stayed. As they did this, their leader shouted to the congregation which was feeling high on drugs;

"Alright, alright, listen to me all of you. Today, we have a special gift and here she comes."

As I perceived of the special gift he was talking about, it was that evil kid-Zuwena whom I have written about in the first chapter. So, amidst the congregational hollering and shouting, smocking bhang and feeling high, Zuwena went up on to the stage. The headman started asking her questions;

"What do you say of Kokote. As you see him, is he a sorcerer?" *"No, he is not."* She answered.

"Well, does he have any medicine upon himself? Let's say any type of charm tied upon his body?"

"No", she answered;

"Is he a devil worshiper?"

"No, I can't judge out." She said.

All this time, the congregation was shouting *"Let him be slaughtered."*

Others were shouting, *"Let him be burned."*

I said,

"Jesus, what is this all about? Who are these people and why do they tie in on me like this?"

Their headman went on to ask Zuwena, *"What is Kokote doing?"*

"He has gone out of that house, knocked at the next door whereby a pastor has welcomed him and they are praying together." She answered.

"Stupid of him" He insulted.

"You all see how foolish he is, he is polluting the air."

He addressed the congregation. At this juncture, I had finished praying with the pastor and had gone back to where I was and laid on the bed. Their headman had become very harsh. Especially at the time when those two messengers had gone back and reported to him that I was not present in my dwelling place. He asked the congregation, ***"Where is he now?"***

One of them answered that I was at my sister's house.

"Why is he unsettled, doesn't he have a home?" He asked as he turned to Zuwena, ***"What is he doing?"***

"He is
polluting
the air

As I knelt down beside the bed to pray, I had come to my senses that I should pray because I was dealing with spiritually evil entities. The headman had become furious. He uttered a command to the same messengers;

"Go right now to his sister's house, get him whether he likes it or not. Bring him here. We are tired of him. We want to hear it from him as to why he does all this".

Dear reader, this was when I found myself gather together and by the power of the Spirit of God and in Jesus mighty name, I jerked off the bed and started rebuking all the power of Satan and that whole congregation. As I called upon the fire of God to come down unto that congregation and consume them in Jesus' mighty name, this really happened. I perceived of the fire of God truly come down in a rage. That congregation became totally confused. As I went on rebuking them, I so surely heard Satan's strongholds being destroyed by Jesus. I really heard some eruptions as bombshells in that Satan's evil stronghold.

It was fire all over that place and I perceived that, Zuwena had become totally destroyed. The headman had become totally pacified as he was being fought on. Everything had become quiet as that whole congregation was dumb founded.

At that point, those two messengers had gone back to their already confused leader and reported about their mission;

"We have been there and we have tried to get him out but it's difficult. We could not touch him because he is being protected by his God."

Then their leader said;

"Well, well, so he pollutes the air but still has his Jesus to protect him? Let him alone." The phrase ***"leave him alone,"*** could have meant a lot to those entities. This is because whenever it was uttered, the war intensified.

Except for their leader-the headman and some few members whom were left at the spot, the rest started scattering everyone to their homes. As he was angry with me and quarreling, I heard a sorceress step forward in front of the others and said; *"Surely, Kokote has overpowered us. I loathe him and I shall surely kill him."* As that congregation dispatched, everyone to their homes, I could hear them as they talked freely. One of them said;

"Kokote has a wonderful and powerful gift. Why then does he like sleeping? And who can tell him not to go on sleeping?"

Another one referring to their headman as a native doctor said;

"You see that native doctor; he lied to us saying that Kokote is a devil worshiper. He also told us that he is weak as he has no food and even has a few clothes. Now have you seen what he did to him and Zuwena?"

The third one answered, *"Nonsense, a gift or no gift ,*

he should be taken to a fellow devil worshipper to be sodomised." Here and there, I could hear doors being opened and closed. I also heard Nyundo come right about my sister's compound and shouted at me. ***"You are better for nothing you fool. We shall burn you under a vehicle tyre."***

That was a new experience for me and it was past midnight. I could not get to sleep so I went on praying and rebuking those evil forces. I was born again but those things were happening too fast for me. At times, I started pondering,

"Jesus, which type of entities am I dealing with. And why are these things happening to me like this?"

At long last I said in my heart, Well, the word of God says,

"I f God is on our side, nobody can be against us. Even hunger nor satisfaction, tribulation nor peace, demons nor angels….. Rom 8: 31-39

No, in all these things we are more than conquerors through Him who loves us."

As I struggled it over, I stood right at my sister's door. There was only a curtain dividing between her room and the kids'. As I prayed and shook with fear, I was standing one foot in my sister's room and the other one in the kids' room as I thought; *"I will run directly into my sister's room for cover if anything physical must happen."*

I kept on praying up to the morning and I was tired. My sister seeing all that I was passing through started to cry. I started comforting her as I told her that I was okay with Jesus on my side as I thought;

"Ah, it's better if she prays rather than cry, she is acting in the flesh rather than in spirit."

Later in the day I said;

"Come what may, I am going back to my house to see how things faired on."

On my way as I walked, I saw a man just seated on a chair outside his house. He said, *"Here he comes and he is going to his house. Doesn't he know that they are looking for him? Now as he goes there, they will get him and kill him straight away."*

I thought; *"well, I will still go there and as a man of God, I should not be a coward."* Rev 21:8 says *"But the fearful, and unbelieving, and the abominable, and murderers, and fornicators, and sorcerers, and idolaters, and liars, shall have their part in the lake which burns with fire and brimstone: which is the second death.* "Mathew 10:28 *"And so do not fear those who kill the body but cannot kill the soul; rather fear Him who can destroy both soul and body in hell."* Still on my way, I heard a woman say; *"You see, no one is ever able to invoke Kokote with sorcery, or demons. He rebukes them on his own and they are out! What type of a person is he?"*

I still went on and just outside the compound, I saw Nyundo and Dama, a young lady and neighbour talking and so I went directly to my house, opened the door and stepped inside. Dama said to Nyundo;

"Did you attend last night's meeting? Did you see what this person did to Zuwena? You see now, that native doctor; He is shying at him and so he can't face him manly enough now. Zuwena had become totally dumb by the power of the fire that this person commanded down. Today, that native doctor is taking her back to Mombasa."

Nyundo answered;

"Well, I did not attend but I was monitoring all the events via a computer in a cyber café. All in all ,he

will be caught by (askari wa mzee) the old man's soldiers."

"Surely, devils have no authority and Kokote should get used to them."Dama noted.

I then thought, *"Well, if they are devils then I should rebuke them over and over in the mighty name of Jesus Christ of Nazareth".*

The following day was on a Sunday and the woman sorcereress was in the forefront. She took the place of Zuwena. As I perceived of it, she was in control. She monitored me through a large computer system.

All throughout the day, I could hear people from the spiritual dark world walking and talking freely about that area. Their destination was always at the control unit. They went there to ask the controller as to what I could be doing. One of them said,

"I am sent to ask by the one who offered the money for Kokote to be killed. He asked as to why that job is still not yet accomplished?"

Then that sorceress and some other two men whom I perceived to be native doctors told her;

"Well, this man is still in the list and we are still trying. He has overpowered us now, and he is always killing some of us, but just pass information to your boss not to worry, we will get him no matter what."

I had already summoned my wife back to Malindi from Mombasa. Since things started, I was still sleeping at my sister's place. Her husband had traveled for another town. However, time to time I went to my house to worship and pray.

Usually, as I went there, the Rastafarians squad with their headman and the rest among that congregation started to come very fast. That congregation was always accompanied by evil powers. As I said my prayers I could hear their leader throwing insults at me saying; *"Kokote is stupid, why does he like polluting the air? If he is clever, why doesn't he have a job and children?"*
Another man suggested; "After *all, he is worshipping his God, let us forgive him and withdraw him from the list."* The headman however answered him; *"Worshiping his God? Don't you see that he is hindering us from doing our work? To hell with him, we shall have to kill him. First of all, we don't want*

him in that house, he has to vacate it and go back to his place of birth Ngao- in Tana Delta and worship his God there. He can't do it here, he is very much stubborn."

The commotion went on outside as I pressed on with my prayers. Most of the time I couldn't see them but perceived them spiritually, talking and doing their things. The controller who was the sorceress' work was always to inform the Rasta's squad and their leaders whenever I started praying. They hated me only for my prayers. Her other work was also to throw some sorcery or Jins to possess me as she monitored me. Whenever she started shooting her sorcery at me, I perceived of it and so I went to my room and started rebuking it off in Jesus' mighty name and I became clear. I realized that whenever she shot some sorcery at me and I was passive, then the war became very harsh against me.

All the forces of darkness became very much clear and too close to me, I felt as someone who was tied and being dragged to hell. As soon as I realized this, I didn't give them a chance; I rebuked all demonic forces to hell in Jesus' mighty name and they were off. I could hear that sorceress complaining; ***"Kokote has out done us; we*** *have tried all we can, but in vain. We can't go on doing our work because he hinders us with his prayers. He is always killing some of us and we are always burying the dead, why should he live? I shall kill him so that he is buried too like our dead members".* Demonic spirits could easily be rebuked and sent to hell. The rest who were normal people (devil worshippers), I was not aware of them at first, and I was circulating that squad studying them not really knowing what to do with them.

As I shot off to church, carrying my bible openly in my hand, I found some two women on the way selling grocery, one of them said; *"He is going to church to burn us."*

As I went on, the other woman said; *"The man of God is going to church to worship God for the last time and after that, he shall be killed. He is not lucky this time round."*

I ignored both of them and went to church. Pastor Malibe, was the preacher that Sunday, after the sermon he gave an alter call for those people who wished to receive Jesus Christ as their personal savior and those who had special needs and wanted to be prayed for. I was among those who went forward who had special needs and as he prayed and rebuked demons, I heard them manifesting one by one and rushing back to hell.

After this the controller/sorceress was nowhere to be found and her place was taken by another woman sorceress. She was accompanied by a man and they were always at the control unit. The other two native doctors, whom were both men, were put aside, however I could perceive of them trying very hard to strike me, but in vain. Some of them from that congregation tried to appear to me as very friendly while others were very brutal, others could say;

"These Rastafarians want to kill the man of God; we surely don't want him to die."

At first, as I called for fire to come down upon them in the mighty name of Jesus Christ, some of them cried; **"Father; Kokote is killing us."**

And I thought;

"Alas! These might be people just like me, and so I might be hurting them!"

I pitied them as, they tightened their grip on me and so I said;

"All right, everyone into the battle field with Jesus as the commander on my side."

The word of God in **_Jeremiah 48:10_** says;

"Cursed be he that doeth the work of the Lord deceitfully, and cursed be he that keeps back his sword from bloodshed."

There was commotion almost every day caused by those evil forces but the biggest fights were fought during the night hours.

My wife had come back to Malindi with Sister Eunia. While Sister Eunia slept in one of the rooms, my wife and I slept in the other room. Usually we could worship and pray before retiring to bed, but I could go on with the prayers after they had retired to bed as I could see the commotion in the spiritual dark world. I could also hear the forces of darkness gathering together.

There was always a meeting on the stage playing on music and raising funds for burials. Some smoked bhang and shouted, while others were beating drums and dancing. As this went on, the DJ changed the whole topic and started hurling insults at me throughout that session.

He was saying;

"Kokote must die for his own foolishness; he has no job and likes polluting the air and sleeping. By the way, I hate these prayerful beggars (watu wa kuombaomba).He has no cloths save for a security trouser he likes wearing. Today he will be brought here and have that uniform stripped off him. He will be whipped and slaughtered in front of everyone here!"

While I laid down in bed, I could hear all this and I said; *"Jesus Christ my Lord, do you hear all these insults and plans against me from the devil?"*

Then I said aloud to that congregation;

"Satan and your fellow demons and satanic spirits together with all your devil agents, you are defeated and have no power over me and my wife in the mighty name of Jesus Christ!"

After praising God, I prayed through **Rev 19:11-16** whereby I asked Jesus to come down as the king of kings wearing white linen turned red and mounting on a white horse. A two sided sharp sword comes out through His mouth. As the Lord Jesus came down in His mighty power, I could perceive of it.

That whole evil congregation could be dumb founded by His mighty power as He descended. Thereafter I asked the Lord to take them on by the sword and the rest were confused.

As their headman was **taken** by the sword off the stage, another person had gone up onto the stage and addressed that congregation;

"All of you have seen what has happened, if Kokote can do such things even asking for fire to come down from heaven, then what next? You have seen how he has started killing some of us and he will be doing it more, he deserves death, that's the only thing that I can say!"

The only thing that amazed me was that, after the Lord had taken that entity (headman) by the sword, I could perceive of him coming back some minutes later.

I didn't know how but every time he was attacked, his strength was being slashed. There was a time whereby he stood in front of me and said;

"Kokote doesn't know that every time he fights me through prayers, I keep on becoming weaker."

This time as he came back, one among the others told him;

"Kokote has locked you in a tin now, he has over powered you."

His voice was drooling as he became weak. He was furious at me as he commanded two people;

"Go tie him hands and feet, drag him here so that we can burn him alive."

As those messengers came, I could hear some dogs barking in front of them. They talked as they came until they got outside the compound. Sometimes I could be lying in bed , but this time I was awake and praying. They were complaining that they could not get me out of the house because I was protected by God. The door might be open or I might be outside for a short call but still they could not be able to get me, so they said;

"We are unable to get him, let's go back and report the matter to the head man."

Usually most pastors think that whenever they rebuke demons out of someone and pray for them, the war is automatically over. Sometimes this is true, but at other times these victims need some counseling and more prayers as the devil is always persistent.

Although he is a defeated foe, he doesn't believe in defeat, he keeps on fighting for a period of time thinking that he will win that person for hell. In all this, I give all glory and honor to God through His only begotten son Jesus Christ. He promised us protection through His word Isaiah 54:17.

"No weapon that is formed against thee shall prosper; and every tongue that shall rise against thee in judgment thou shall condemn. This is the heritage of the servants of the Lord and their righteousness is of me said the Lord."

One memorable morning, as I woke up from sleep, I perceived of a weird thing happening in the spiritual realm. The devil had chained a child by his one leg to the stem of a tree. He boasted that he would soon eat him up. Deeply inside my heart, I felt that it should not happen that way. I then started to pray and got on breaking that chain in the mighty name of Jesus Christ. Abruptly, in the twinkle of an eye, the chain was broken and the child started flying heavenward. The devil violently pursued, caught him up and chained him again. I then said; **"No way Jesus Christ my Lord, why is this happening this way?"**

I again started offering prayers, this time vigorously and continued breaking that chain by faith in Jesus Christ's mighty name. The chain was finally broken and the child flew off heavenward as the devil pursued in vain. The child disappeared off in the sky, probably unto God's heavenly aboard. When he missed getting hold of the child, he descended back to the ground and continued insulting and cursing – Rev 12.

CHAPTER 3

<u>THE GATHERING OF THE EVIL</u>

One day, Sister Eunia sent me to the town to see someone: I didn't refuse as I was always being threatened by those evil entities that whenever I said I would go to town, they would swear to net me there and kill me.

In this situation I said; ***"Well, I am a child of God and I shall not fear the devil and his evil forces."*** So, off I went to town and as I walked along, I heard a lot of demonic voices coming through the air. I perceived that there were tall and unseen buildings on the way as those voices were flowing through unseen windows.

A feminine demonic voice said to me; ***"I surely love you, but you are unlovable."***

She seemed to shy off as she said it. I felt disgusted and so I said to her;

"Listen you devil, I don't love you; I love Jesus Christ my Lord, so you are defeated in the mighty name of Jesus Christ of Nazareth."

I commanded them off as I kept on walking. While outdoors, I always made sure that there were no people near me as I commanded off those devils for they might mistake me for being crazy.

Once in town, the war almost doubled. It was 1:30 pm, day time and I heard a proclamation from a temple. It blared through loudspeakers as I almost froze from within with fear and I said; ***"Fear, get off me in Jesus' mighty name."***

I said this as I kept moving while the proclamation blared on;

"Now we want our esteemed government to take Kokote to account for his own misdeeds.

He is always killing innocent people just like that without any care. Why should he aim his fighting gadgets at fellow citizens? The government should look for a way of eliminating him, as it is, he deserves a death sentence."

As that drama went on, I looked for a strategic place whereby I sat as I waited for that person I was sent to see. On the opposite side from where I sat, there were three Giriama men also seated.

They wore white and long (gowns). They sat calmly as they talked in low voices about me. I could see them clearly and hear them audibly say;

"Kokote is clever, and what makes him shine like this? I guess its holiness, look at him, he is uneasy and may start running."

One of them replied and said; *"He won't run."*

I thought; *"Well, this is the seat of Prophet Elijah that he sat on just to prove that the Lord is able and thereafter, executed four hundred and fifty prophets of Baal."1 Kings 18:20-40.*

I sat on the same, this time just to prove whether it's Jesus Christ or my legs that were more able.

The seat was too hot until I felt my legs faintly starting to give way, knock together and blow the whistle such that the race could start at once.

Thanks to Jesus Christ my Lord who made me to stick right there. I was sweating profusely as I thought;

"Fiddle sticks, the police will break loose at any time just to net me for judgment."

I then saw another person, probably the one whom proclaimed through that temple. He was a distant away and he said;

"We are not able to make Kokote run, it's difficult, let's only oppress him!"

The whole situation was disturbing as the one I awaited took decades to appear. I decided to start walking back home. On my way back, I heard people praying earnestly for me in a church. They prayed on saying; *"Dear, Lord, protect the life of Kokote."*

They prayed on and on via loudspeakers. One man prayed a prophetic prayer while a woman translated it.

I thought and said to myself;

"Jesus, what is your will in all this? And what does all this mean? Who sent my name to this church? I don't understand any of this!"

Foot and hand as I walked on, I could perceive of a meeting being conducted in a storey building.

The headman was the one briefing that congregation and so he said to them;

"Well, I have all Kokote's records with me on my table. He is a foolish person who cannot work. He has no children and before he sleeps, he pollutes the air. However, I warn you of him, he is a mature

born again Christian, as you go for him, be careful. Right now I want two people to go right out there, tie his hands and feet and drag him here."

I mused in my mind saying; *"The Lord is on my side and so it's simple and clear, nothing and no one can be against me." Romans 8:31-39*

The ones sent came and failed so they went back to report.

I arrived at home and there, I found pastor peter, Sister Eunia and my wife. As we sat there talking, I could expressly hear that meeting going on. Later, I perceived that they stood up and started to pray to their god the devil (Lucifer). *"Father, let Kokote the devil worshipper be defeated in the name of Jesus,"*

My fellow companions didn't know what was going on so I stood up excusing myself and off I went to my room. I closed the door behind me as I addressed those entities;

"Listen, you Satan and all your fellow demonic spirits plus all your evil agents together with your Jesus. You are the ones whom shall kneel down before my Lord Jesus Christ and confess that He is Lord to God's glory."

I started praying through the word of God according to **Jeremiah 23:29** which says, ***"Is not my word like fire? Says the Lord and like a hammer which breaks the rock in pieces?"***

In Jesus' mighty name, I asked for the word of God as a hammer to strike them and they started crying; ***"Father Kokote is oppressing us."***

One day as we prayed and went to bed, the fight was on. The man and woman wizards were on the monitoring unit. Wherever I might be, those two wizards would put their monitoring gadgets/stronghold one or two houses away.

Whatever I would be doing, especially if I prayed, those two communicated the matter to their head man. However, I found them to be a bridge for the others to come and go as they pleased .I started telling Jesus that whether they were devil worshippers or familiar spirits, I didn't need them.

Always, as they would tell on me that I was praying, I could perceive of the whole Rastafarians group and their leader coming very fast in their pickup. They always carried large loudspeakers in their vehicle with some music system.

Their leader was always full of insults and anger. From time to time he would stop to play some music. As they came, I usually heard children shouting and playing about them.

The whole scene was like one whereby a witchdoctor comes to a village masquerading as one with the power to net out sorcerers from within that area. Usually, the out raged villagers take the law into their hands. They beat those said to be sorcerers to death. Sometimes they parade their victims all along the roads as they beat them up shouting.

Most of them would likely be children in the forefront shouting. At times the police could come in between and save those people. During those occasions as they came, they usually put their evil stronghold some distance away.

Those two wizards would then straight away go to persuade them to go back.

They always told them;

"Leave, Kokote alone! He has not yet polluted the air again. You may now go and come back for him immediately if he pollutes the air."

Their headman would say; **"I love him so much but he**

is unlovable. I would like to sodomize him especially if he pollutes the air. First of all, we want to tarnish him a sorcerer so that we will get him and kill him."

As those two wizards got back to their post, leaving those Rastafarians at their position, a lot of children could be playing around my house. As I perceived of it, I could always hear them playing about as they insulted me. They would say; ***"We are waiting to see this sorcerer as he is executed."***

As those two wizards came, they always persuaded them,

"Now, you kids go back home and leave Kokote alone. He has not yet polluted the air."

I then turned to those two wizards and said; "You two wizards. Whether you are familiar spirits or devil worshipers, I don't need you. Be defeated in the mighty name of Jesus Christ."

They were furious, especially the man. He said,

"Kokote is really a fool. We are helping him and he doesn't appreciate. He needs someone to send him to the real place to see demons confused and scattering as he prays and rebukes them. Surely devils have no authority. But now see, he says that he

doesn't want us."

All through that night I perceived of another woman entity. She masqueraded as a higher personality in sorcery. She commanded more evil power and vigor than the headman. She put up an evil stronghold somewhere nearby and all the others gathered around her.

They had a meeting as those two wizards and that squad of Rastafarians held into their positions a little bit far from them. People were reporting to her of how difficult it was to get me.

Others said; *"He is a born again Christian and we also think that he has a gift"*

She answered, *"Well, I don't think of him having a gift but he has favor from God. However, we shall have to devise some means and ways to get him."*

That woman entity that I give the name Melisa seemed to be truly evil. She had a disgusting evil commanding voice and she said; *"There is no any other alternative; Kokote has to be eliminated and very fast at that."*

I shook my wife, *"Lois, get up you know we need must pray", "Agh! J.K we have already prayed by faith. Let us sleep"* She said. *"Well done."* I thought. *"It's only the one whom has been bitten by a snake and so whenever he sees a rope, he leaps."*

I had some anointing oils and so, I woke up and put only one spoonful of it in a jar of water. I asked the Lord Jesus Christ to intervene and make it to be the true blood of Jesus. I anointed the doors, windows and the rest I threw over the top of the roof.

As I did this, those two wizards said; *"Kokote is very clever. He is anointing the place with oil. Surely devils have no authority as you will see what will arise from this act. He seems to be a teacher when he does these things."*

I went back and lay on my bed as usual. I could not get any sleep so I kept on perceiving of the events as they uncovered in the spiritual realm. Sometimes I used some pure water and the outcome was swift. It's just a matter of faith. The word of God says that Elijah was a man like us and he prayed -James 5:17-18 *"Elijah was a man of like nature with ourselves and he prayed fervently that it might not rain, and for three and a half years it did not rain on the earth. Then he prayed again and the heaven gave rain, and the earth brought forth its fruits."* Melisa was by then in a furious mood as she had heard all that pertained of me as told by that evil congregation. She seemed to be on a throne as the others gathered around her. She commanded two people to come to where I was and take me by force. As they came, I could hear some dogs barking in front of them. Those were dogs that could bark and talk simultaneously as human beings. They came as they talked. Three to four minutes, they were right at the spot.

They said;

"It's difficult to get him. Let us wait until he sleeps and we will then get him out."As this went on, I slept and as I woke up, I heard them still there as they said, "His God loves him the most especially as he goes to sleep. Let us go back and report."

They went back and reported to Melisa whom became much angrier.

She said;

"Well, I will go there on my own and see him come out whether he likes it or not."

The man wizard was the one whom went there and escorted her to my place. This was the man, whom always said, **"Surely devils have no authority."**

As they reached some few meters away from my place. Melisa was pointing a finger at the house in confusion asking;

"And what is that? Isn't it blood? Surely, it's blood. How does this person worship God?"

She repeated those words as she turned around, running towards her evil stronghold. The man didn't run, he went to where his counterpart was. Suddenly, the Rastafarians and their leader got confused.

Their leader repeated the same words as did Melisa; **"Oh, how does this person worship his God?"**

He said this as they also ran towards Melisa's evil stronghold. All through that night, they kept trying to capture me in vain as I kept on praying.

During the day time, Sister Eunia sent me to the law courts in the town to see someone. Along the way, I saw someone riding on a bicycle. He looked at me until he passed by and turned to stare at me.

He chuckled and said;

"Hehehe! The person himself is very cool. He also seems to be polite, but wait until when he prays

and see him command down real fire."

Still, as I strode on, I saw two other people talking, ***"Surely this person is a threat. Whenever he prays, you just see his master appear. Sometimes you might think that He is just a mere man but coming with great power. Everyone shoots off into the forest."*** The other one said, ***"Well, Kokote maybe an angel and we might be fighting with him, just for nothing."***

The Rastafarians with their leader were following me from my back. They were always in their pickup. The headman kept on shouting and threatening me wherever I turned. I kept on rebuking them silently. They were invisible but as I got to the town, I saw some of them with their white pickup manifested. They were Rastafarians and they packed it on the road side. They were on the pavement saluting one another in a fashion they know how. One of them said,

"This person is surely great. He can't be touched by us." As they manifested, they didn't radiate any ***brutality. Sometimes, they might be seated somewhere as they said, "Kokote, look at us. We are here."***

I ignored them all as I went to the law court office. I

entered into the said office and enquired of the person in question. I was told that he was out for lunch and he would soon come back. In the office, there was a secretarial woman and other two women and a man.I chose to sit outside as I perceived of the secretary telling the others of all the events as they happened,

"Well, on the first day, Kokote did it himself. He prayed until a strange thing happened. He destroyed that kid with his prayers. Sometimes he does it on his own and at other times he goes to some pastors and gets them to pray for him."

I kept on sitting there as it seemed to take decades for that person to appear. As I waited, I saw some three Swahili men wearing their long white aprons. They were on my right hand side but later on, they shifted to my front side.

They stared at me as they talked in low voices; ***"Kokote is clever, and probably its holiness that makes him shine like this."***

I didn't want to concern myself about them .So I concentrated on waiting for the person in question. When he came, I finished with him and started going back home.

Something amazed me so much. Whenever I strolled about that town, I could hear cassettes being played on as a repetition about what might have happened the previous night.

The cassettes contained of all the nightly events from the beginning up to the time I prayed and the power of God destroyed the Rastafarian's strong holds. They were played in shops, in barber shops, in houses and in many other places. I wondered as to how the devil could do all this recording about his own down fall.

CHAPTER 4

<u>EVERY KNEE SHALL BOW DOWN</u>

One memorable night, that evil congregation gathered as normal. I could perceive of them smocking bhang, shouting and feeling high. Melisa and their headman were present. We had already prayed and gone to bed.

As that congregation started conducting their usual ceremonies, I did not give them a chance.

I knelt down and called upon the power of God to come down from heaven. As the fire came down, I perceived of it. I immediately asked the Lord Jesus to take Melisa and their head man by that fire.

They were hurled up and round by the fire as they poured insults at me. They were held up in the sky by the Lord Jesus for almost half an hour. After that, they were let down.

They were panting and Melisa was wrath with me. She said, **"You see now what Kokote has done to my house? He has burned it down and so I can't forgive him for that. He shall have to pay me for the** *damages."*

Others said, *"How will a person whom doesn't have a job pay you?"* She answered;

"Well, then we will tarnish him and say that he is a devil worshipper and then kill him."

I said, *"My dear Lord, Jesus Christ, You have heard what they said? How can I be asked to pay for house destruction? How can I present myself in front of such a weird congregation? Jesus Christ my Lord, you are the one who did it and you certainly know how to finish off this game."*

I also prayed to God and said, *"My dear heavenly father in the mighty name of Jesus, I command this evil congregation from the dark world to kneel down before Jesus and with their own mouths confess that He is Lord. Let them also know and confess with their own mouths that I am God's servant in Jesus' mighty name."*

As all that happened, the others broke off to their homes. There was a certain night, that evil congregation gathered together as usual. There were also a lot of children among them. The D.J was on the stage as usual feeding the others with weird music.

In a minute, he stopped the music and called upon a kid on to the stage.

He said;

"Do you all see how Kokote has burned this kid? He is truly a fool. I want some two people right now to go for him and get him here so that he may pray for her to get to normal."

There and then, I knelt down and prayed,

"Jesus Christ my Lord, can I really go to such a weird meeting to pray for people from the dark side of the world? You can even hear their headman as he hurls insults at me. Let him have a padlock put upon his mouth in Jesus' mighty name. Let him also kneel down in Jesus' name and confess that Jesus is king of kings."Philippians 2:10.

Immediately, I perceived of him having the padlock upon his mouth as he was forced to kneel down. Though he had the padlock put on him, he still radiated a lot of pride as he forced insults out through the sides of his mouth. Psalms 10:7-11. I also perceived of some two great forces flying out of him.

The others were dumb founded as they shouted in awe. After that, the other members broke off to their homes.

Melisa appeared onto the stage and said;

"Do you see what Kokote has done to the headman? How can he go on like this with a padlock upon his mouth? Two people right now to go there and drag him here so that he may pray for him to get well again."

I said; *"Jesus Christ my Lord, you did this, you know what to do about such fights."* I said this as I sneaked to sleep. He was held on like that as he struggled up to the time he was released.

 He went on becoming weak as he was always fought. One day I perceived of him stand in front of me as he had taken up the position of a Giriama witchdoctor.

He said; *"Kokote has surely overpowered me. Every time he prays and rebukes me, I become weaker and so now our strengths are equal. Let the fight be between me and him."*

I said; *"Listen you devil, the war must be fought between you versus my master Jesus Christ."*

My wife and sister Eunia had gone back to Mombasa. They had gone because I had convinced them that things were not so bad. By then, those dark forces were threatening me so much that I should vacate the house, leave Malindi and go to Ngao to worship my God there.

One day, as that Rastafarian squad came for me in their pickup as a result of my prayers, I thought;

"Jesus Christ my Lord, what do I do to these?"

I then did what the prophet Elisha did to those Syrians. First of all I asked the Lord Jesus Christ to strike them with blindness - 2kings 6:8-23.

I then said to them;

"The man you are looking for is not here in Malindi. He is in Kilifi, go to Kilifi and look for him there."

At once, they shot off to Kilifi to look for me there. I stayed at home pruning the fence and as I prayed in the afternoon, they arrived with a pomp in their white pickup. They were complaining that I had lied to them as I told them that I was not the man they wanted. They were also insisting that I should vacate the place. At that time, I went inside my room, closed the door behind me and said to them;

"Listen you Satan and your fellow demonic spirits and all your evil agents. I will not follow your commands, but I will follow my masters (Jesus) commands. If it's Him who says I should go home then I will go. But as for you, I rebuke you in the mighty name of Jesus."

I decided to go to a certain place whereby I used to work for a period of time to ask them for my pay.

I went there purporting in my heart that I would be going to Mombasa and never to my place of birth.

As I went to that place, that whole squad with their headman kept on following me from my back.

They kept on shouting, insulting and threatening me as I walked on.

I got into the office as I was told to try again the following week. As I came out of that office, all the forces of darkness had surrounded me.

A demonic spirit from the sky said,

"Alas, they are oppressing Kokote for nothing. He is a good person and we don't want him to die".

Another said; ***"Oh, I pity him. First of all, he has no job and no money. How can he even be able to board a bus? He even has no cloths and no food at home. They are ill-treating him for nothing."***

Then their headman said; ***"Ok, Kokote, whether you have money or no money, we don't want you to ever set your feet in that house again. Now turn around and start going on foot towards Tana Delta."***

I didn't say a word but, I looked for a nearby church, got inside and started –praying and rebuking those evil forces. They stopped outside as they hurled insults and shouted at me – 2 Chronicles 6:28-31.They raged with fury as they could not be able to touch me. After that I said I would go and sleep at home come what may. Before I could go home, I set my mind to go to pastor Peter's house.

As I walked on, that squad followed me from behind as they shouted at me and complained;

"It's difficult to kill him. What do we do then?" Another suggested, ***"We will get him through the screen. We will stub him with a knife through the screen and he will fall dead, let's go."***

Suddenly, they all disappeared at once. At pastor Peter's house, he offered me a seat as I narrated the ordeal to him. I told him that I was in a bad mood and I would like to be with him as we passed the night together in my house.

He accepted as he asked me to accompany him somewhere and thereafter we could go to my place.

At the agreed place, pastor Peter got inside a house to see someone as I remained outside. It was around seven p.m. the situation had become worse.

Their headman/Satan came alone this time as he stood face to face with me. He was furious as he addressed me;

"I have told you to go to Ngao but you have refused. You want to go and sleep in that house by force. You think that you are clever? Don't think that you will be made to be our member of parliament. Go and sleep there and you will surely see."

Pastor Peter was out and we went home. We prayed earnestly and then got to bed to sleep. That night, I had taken some sleep pills. We slept well and at around midnight,

I was terribly woken up by what I felt like a knife stub

through my side ribs. I jerked up at once as I bent over sideways, holding my ribs with my hand. This was not physical but I could feel the pain going in through my ribs and I started to pray and rebuke those evil forces at once.

As I jerked up, I perceived of a large audience shouting and saying,

"Oh no, he has killed the servant of God."

"Yes, I have done my work. I have done it." He boasted.

I kept on praying and rebuking those evil forces as I started feeling o.k. They then held a big meeting as their headman kept on sending people to get me. As they went to report that they could not be able to touch me, their headman said;

"Right now, I want two of you to go to Mombasa and get his wife. She is a devil worshipper and he doesn't know about it. We will then sacrifice her straight away."

I didn't like that idea so I shook and woke up the pastor. I told him about the ordeal as I said;

"Please, let us pray for my wife Lois."

He told me that I should not worry as we had already prayed by faith. He then told me to go and keep on sleeping as the Lord was in charge.

I thought; ***"Well done, I will keep on praying for her."***

So I let Pastor Peter go on sleeping as I kept fighting it out in prayers. Two to three minutes later, those messengers had arrived in Malindi from Mombasa.

They reported the issue; ***"His wife is also untouchable. We tried and failed. He loves his wife and so he has covered her with prayers and that's why we could not get to her."***

He would say;

"You say he loves her but she is a devil worshipper. When he sleeps with her, he does it with a snake. Go get him here for he is also a devil worshipper. We will slaughter him just now".

I said;

"Satan, you are a liar and the father of lies. Be defeated in the mighty name of Jesus Christ."

John 8:44

I kept on praying as I heard a commotion emanating from the midst of that evil congregation.

I heard a child crying sarcastically as it was being sacrificed. I also perceived of a woman crying as she was prepared to be sacrificed also. My heartfelt faint as I kept on praying and rebuking those evil forces in the mighty name of Jesus Christ.

CHAPTER 5

<u>THE WAR IN THE SKY</u>

There was a certain night whereby that congregation had gathered as their usual norm. I knelt down and started praying and praising the Lord. Thereafter, I called for fire from heaven to come down in Jesus' mighty name.

As the fire came down, I perceived of it and so I called upon Jesus to take on Melisa and their headman. They were immediately hurled up and around, scorched by the fire as they shot insults at me. There was a dreadful hovering sound in the sky as they were pushed around and around.

The others were looking on as those two wizards came from the monitoring unit and I said,

"Jesus, let those two entities plus all the others confess that you are Lord and that I am your servant."

Those two wizards used their own means and pulled Melisa down.

They told her;

"Kokote is not a devil worshipper. He is a servant of

God. His God doesn't want anyone to call him a devil worshipper. Come on, change your tactic and start calling him a servant of God."

As they left her, she was hurled up in the circus. She started proclaiming,

"Kokote is a servant of God, leave him alone."

As she kept saying good things about me, she was released from the circus. While she was among the others, she changed her attitude completely from a raging figure to a sympathizing being.

She kept on telling the others that I was a servant of God and I was persecuted for nothing.

She also teamed with those other two wizards and presented themselves to me as good friends.

I didn't need them either and so the fight was on.

They used the same method to pull down their headman as they told him to do what Melisa had done. He refused and so he was hurled up and around as he was probed with fire. He was shouting saying that he would not relent until he killed me.

There was a big fight in the sky. It started from three

am to six a.m. My wife had come back to Malindi and we were lying on our bed.

I asked her;

"Do you hear what is going on outside in the sky? May we go out and see what God is doing to those ilfrits?"

She said, **"No, I still feel sleepy so let us sleep."**

There was another night whereby, I perceived of those evil forces gathering together. There was that squad of Rastafarians that was always in the forefront. They were feared the most by the others.

As they gathered there with the exception of their leader, I started to pray. I then asked the Lord Jesus to impart the gifts of the Holy Spirit in them.

Immediately and to my astonishment, I heard them speaking in other tongues as they prophesied.

A few minutes later, their leader arrived outside, shocked as he asked;

"What has this fool done to these people?"

Before he could go on hurling insults at me, I asked the

Lord Jesus Christ to impart in him the same gifts of the Holy Spirit. To my amazement, he started to prophesy. He went among the others inside a temple and started prophesying in Kiswahili. He kept on prophesying a lot of good things about God and me. 1Samuel 19:18-24 as I thought;

"Jesus Christ my Lord, how can this happen to a weird squad like this? How can it happen in the spiritual realm and not in the physical realm?"

The others among that congregation were outside that temple talking freely.

One of them said;

"Do you see this native doctor who always insults the man of God? Today he is only prophesying good things about him with his own lips."

In some few minutes, Melisa arrived at the spot. She was furious and she said;

"What does this mean? Who has given Kokote the authority to pray for devils to receive the gifts of the Holy Spirit? Stupid of him, I will kill him."

Sometimes I heard Bongo music played on praising me as

they mentioned my name. In the message, they also said that Kokote beats them (devils) as he wishes. I wondered as to whom has given those dark forces the authority to sing about me.

I said, *"You dark forces, with your music strong hold, are defeated in the mighty name of Jesus."*

There was a certain night whereby I called upon the Lord in **Rev: 19: 11-16** to take on that entire congregation. Melisa and their headman were immediately hurled up in the sky as they poured insults at me. The others were fought on the ground level. After the war was over, I heard them panting as they scattered everyone to their homes.

As they walked along, one of them said; *"Kokote has surely out done us."*

Another one said;

"This person doesn't want development. Why can't he let alone those who want this development?

We can no longer do our work just because he hinders us."

One night as that congregation gathered together

with the exception of their leader, I asked the Lord Jesus to impart the gifts of the Holy Spirit in them. To my amazement, I heard them at once praying aloud in tongues. I said, **"Jesus Christ my Lord, what is the meaning of all this?"** Immediately, their leader arrived at the place and he was furious.

He said; *"What does this mean? That God is among this congregation? Kokote is not lucky this time, I will kill him."* One day, pastor Malibe with some other members of the church; were at the market place making a pulpit for a crusade.

The crusade was to be held the following day. I went to him and told him to pray for me as those things had become worse. He told me that he was busy and that I should go to the crusade the following day.

It was around 6pm and so I took a chair and sat down.

There was a group of around four grown up people in the field playing on with a ball. They then stared at me as one of them said;

"Kokote is wobbling just for nothing. He has out done the devils already and now he wants that pastor to pray for him."

There were also some children playing as one of them told the others.

"Did you see that old man in the temple jumping over the fire and almost fell? This is the person who commanded down that fire."

I thought,

"Fiddle sticks! I have come for prayers and these people are just bickering. O.k., I am going back home and I will fight these evil forces by the power of Jesus Christ. No matter the outcome."

The following afternoon as I sat among others at the crusade listening to the Sermon, I could perceive of voices bickering about me.

They said;

"These Rastafarians are oppressing Kokote for nothing. He is a man of God. He has come here to have prayers by his pastor but still, he has the power to carry the whole of a church on his shoulders. He can be a good pastor."

I ignored them all and stayed there for prayers. Another time as I prayed inside my house, their headman came very fast and stopped outside. He had a Sub-machine gun in his hands and so he started to shoot;

"Bang! Bang! Bang! I will kill Kokote if ever he persists to sleep in this house."

Someone else said; *"Slow down my man, you know there are other people here."*

I prayed on ignoring them completely. I had also let open all doors and windows as I did it the way of Daniel 16:10.

One afternoon, I went to my local church for prayers. I went there to pray on my own. This was a day for the choir practice. They played the keyboard as they sang choruses. They were on the pulpit facing my direction as I was alone in the back row.

As they sang choruses, I kept on praying and binding those evil forces. They started manifesting one after the other as they went to hell. Everything had become cool except for the choir that went on singing. Immediately, I perceived of a squad from the dark kingdom right from behind my back.

They said; *"Well done Kokote. Surely no one can kill you that easily. You just look at us;*

we are right behind you."

I chose to ignore them as I kept on praying. After that, I went home.

One day, pastor peter with his assistant pastor asked me to accompany them somewhere. At the said place, they entered inside a house as I sat outside waiting. In front of me, there was another house whereby a squad of around seven young stars sat on a bench.

They kept on bickering;

"Here is the man of God, and you see that pastor he has accompanied? He is not stronger in faith than him. The other man is a devil worshipper and Kokote doesn't know this. We haven't seen a man like Kokote in the whole of this place. His God loves him and answers him for whatever he prays for. He seems to be the only one going to heaven."

Another one said;

"Hey guys, remember what we had been told in the meeting? We were told to give him total respect. Let's leave him alone."

Something else started to happen every day in the

morning hours. I could hear sorcerers, witchdoctors and demonic spirits hovering in the sky from two am up to six am in the morning.

They soared freely in the sky as though in aero planes as they talked. They conducted their evil activities from the sky as they soared on.

I shook my wife;

"Sweety, wake up and let's pray. You know there are evil activities going on in the sky."

She said; ***"Let us sleep and don't let the devil scare you."***

I thought,

"Well, I have to pray on, come what may." I kept on rebuking them as I called for fire from heaven to strike them in Jesus' mighty name. To my amazement, they started falling down in bunches.

They were confused as I could hear them talking, walking and scattering everyone to their homes.

In some other nights, I could also hear a demonic spirit hovering in the air in around two to three minutes before 3 a.m. He then jumped inside a temple and started to proclaim the greatness of God.

In one of the nights, I timed him as he soared on and I started to rebuke him in Jesus' mighty name. He stepped into the temple, did his stuff and thereafter, he came out in a rage, and I could perceive of him face me and say;

"You think that its only your religion that is Godly but others' are demonic. You are not lucky this time, I will kill you."

There was a certain night as those evil forces had gathered together as their headman went on spitting fire, with rage. One among that congregation told him,

"You say that Kokote doesn't have a job and also likes polluting the air and sleeping; why can't you try giving him a job? Try him and see whether he can work or not."

He answered;

"Well if you think so, I will ask from (the penguin broadcasting co-operation) name withheld to give him a big job and a smart car."

I was in my house as I faced towards that evil

congregation and I said;

"Listen to me you Satan and your fellow demonic spirits and all of you sorcerers and witchdoctors. I will never accept any job or any gift offered by you. The word of God says that wealth and prosperity comes from the Lord Proverbs: 8:18-21. I rebuke you in the mighty name of Jesus."

Sometimes the devil used radio stations (spiritually) in fighting me. I could always hear some debates going on in those radio stations as I was the centre of concentration. I could hear people asked as to what they could suggest done to a person like me. Others suggested that I should be killed.

I kept on rebuking those strongholds of the devil and they were defeated. At a certain time, Melisa was being asked questions in one of those radio stations as she answered all about me.

There was the broadcaster and some other two men with Melisa in that station. I immediately started praying and rebuking them in Jesus' mighty name. At once, I heard Melisa let out a loud cry in anguish.

I kept rebuking until I was over with it. In the town, and

everywhere I heard evil voices

saying, *"The Rastafarians want to bribe the man of God today, they want to give him a job with the penguin broadcasting co-operation. They also want to give him a car."*

Another one said; *"They will not be able to bribe him. He is a born again Christian and so he can't accept to become a devil worshipper."*

At night as I lay on my bed, I could hear that evil congregation gathering in a meeting. Their headman addressed them with a pure Giriama accent. On that day, he also posed as a great Giriama native doctor. He conducted the meeting as he said;

"Kokote is a servant of God and we love him. Today we have talked to the penguin broadcasting co-operation to give him a job and a car. I want two people to go to his house and call him here o.k. go."

On the stage, there was the voice of a well-known radio broadcaster. She kept on saying,

"Kokote, we know that you are a servant of God. No one wants to hurt you.

Don't refuse to come so that you may have the job and the car given to you."

Those messengers had already reached outside my compound. They were using their own weird formulae to woe me out of the house.

They also kept on complaining.

"We can't get him out. It's difficult because he is covered."

I said; ***"Listen you Satan! I don't accept a job or gifts from you. Be defeated in the Mighty name of Jesus Christ."***

The devil is a liar. Sometimes he might use someone you know to frustrate you. A person might be talking one thing and the devil might cause another voice to backfire from him talking bad things about you. If you face such a person, he might be dumbfounded because he might not know what you are after.

He always wants people to hate one another just for nothing. This is an area that the devil always uses to take people captives.

There was once a sister Ruth (name withheld) whom

always complained that there were people who talked about her and insulted her.

Sometimes she could spill some dirty water through the window of her house to people just seated and talking outside. She would say that they were talking evil about her.

I advised her that as she is born again, she should start fighting spiritually by praying not physically. That was if she sees or hears people talking about her, she should start rebuking those evil forces just through prayers.

Surely, the devil wanted to bribe me with a job and a car just for me to forgo my salvation. There is a proverb that people say about him that, "***The devil offers no free gifts.***"

I faced him and said;

"Satan, I can't accept your gifts. The bible says esteem and wealth comes from the Lord proverbs 8:18-21.So be defeated in the mighty name of Jesus

CHAPTER 6

<u>THE VIDEO SHOW</u>

There was a certain night whereby I slept well and later on, I was woken up by a great commotion from the dark world. There was a big shout from one of the greatest congregation I had never heard before.

The devil was present and was showing that evil congregation a video show. The show was a collection of all the events of the spiritual war fare that was being fought and won over by Jesus Christ.

Everyday's events were shown. Even, as I called for fire from heaven to come down and take them on in Jesus' mighty name.

As the events uncovered, the commotion was great while that shocked congregation shouted in awe.

Then the devil said;

"These are the shocking things that Kokote is performing. One can imagine about how many

damages he would have caused by the time he is caught. Come on, two people go get him."

I woke up with a start. I asked the Lord God for intervention in this and then I

said; *"Dear heavenly Father let the devil plus the whole of this evil congregation be sent to a faraway place. As they get there, let a large wall of fire of the Holy Spirit stand between them and me. Dear Lord, let me be surrounded by eternal peace from you in Jesus' name."*

At once, they were carried off to a faraway place from me and the atmosphere became cool. However, other lesser dark forces which were not in that congregation were striding here and there as they talked.

I can say that my name was known and mentioned by almost everyone from the spiritual dark world. They mentioned it freely as though they knew me even as from when I was born.

During the days of Zuwena, a woman asked her whether what I had was a gift or not.

"I don't know." She said. "It will only be a gift if he passes the test, but will he pass really? He will just

die." In the book of James 1:12, the word of God says; "Blessed is the man who endures trial, for when he has stood the test he will receive the crown of life which God has promised to those who love him."

In a certain night, as that congregation gathered together, I asked the Lord Jesus Christ to let his voice thunder among them as in psalms 29. As it thundered, I heard them complaining.

Their headman said;

"We are surely tired of Kokote. See what he is doing, why can't he leave us alone?"

I said; *"No Satan, you are a liar and you are defeated in the mighty name of Jesus*

Christ." John 8:44

They might always say that I should leave them alone, but as they gathered, they devised on new ways of attacking me. That was why I never wanted to give them a chance.

Sometimes as they could have used local sorcerers and witchdoctors to hurt me and failed, so they could also hire other superior than they, let's say from Tanzania etc. Those ones also failed terribly under the power and the name of Jesus. During one of those terrible nights, that evil congregation gathered as usual. They had hired the help of some two sorceresses as their special guests.

They had come from another country probably to try their luck in hurting me. They started to set up their evil strongholds so that they might start to attack me as I said;

"Jesus Christ my Lord, I need your intervention in this. Don't let them prevail in this."

I then started to ask for fire from heaven to come down upon them in Jesus' Mighty name.

As the fire came down, I perceived of it as I said;

"You sorcerers, I rebuke you and your evil strongholds. Be destroyed by the fire from heaven in Jesus' mighty name"

As I kept rebuking them, I perceived of both of them plus a few of others among that evil congregation thrown down by the power of God. I could also perceive of their evil strongholds erupting as though fired by bombshells.

Someone among them whom I thought was not their headman said; **"Kokote is dangerous. See what he has** *done. He has knocked people down."*

He said this as he went towards one of the women; *"Get up mama, get up mama."*

Then they conducted a quick and urgent meeting.

That man said;

"What do we do with Kokote? We are tired of him as he keeps on hindering us from doing our work."

Someone else answered;

"Well, let us clear him off the list. Let us forgive him that he is a servant of God and after all he is worshipping his God."

The man said;

"You say that we forgive him? Don't you see that whenever he worships his God, he keeps on cutting off our strongholds? Fuck him up, I will kill him."

One day, at around six pm, as I started to worship, those two wizards from the monitoring unit had communicated about it to their headman. The headman plus that special group held first near him were those Rastafarians.

This squad was the most feared among that evil congregation. So as they got the information, they started to come very fast in their pickup.

I faced those two wizards and said,

"Alright, today let them come and they will face what Dathan and Korah had faced before Moses and Haron and the rest of the Israelites." Numbers 16:25-34. Those two did not communicate about that issue to that squad. They kept saying, "Surely, devils have no authority. Why can't Kokote pray for us? We can be very much pleased if he prays for us."

As that squad came, they grew very much angry with me as they found me praying. They had a whole Music set in their pick up with large speakers. Their headman started to shout at me and I told him;

"Let you be punished with all the curses and diseases of Egypt in Jesus' Mighty name." And he fell there wriggling on the ground.

I also said,

"Dear Lord Jesus Christ let this Rastafarian squad face what Dathan and Korah faced. Let the ground open up and envelop them." The whole of that evil

squad fell in and were covered by the ground.

The others among that congregation stood aside. There was some confusion and another person got onto the stage. He was also a rapper as he played music and rapped.

Things were mixed up as those two wizards from the monitoring unit went to report the issue to another superior squad. I was still rebuking them and as they arrived, I found myself there also in the spirit as I went around and around them looking for a way to attack them.

The two reported the issue,

"The servant of God had commanded the ground to open up and all the Rastafarians went down- buried."

That superior squad consisted of three male figures. One of them asked, *"And what of the headman?"*

*"He also perished:"*They answered. I kept on going round and round rebuking them as I could see and hear some eruptions around them. They seemed to have caged themselves in one way or the other as they said;

"Ah, leave off your stuff. Do you think that we can be destroyed so much easily like the rest?"

I said;

"Well, you are nothing to Jesus and one day, he will still destroy you."Jeremiah: 1:8-10 "Be not afraid of their faces for I am with thee to deliver thee', said the Lord. Then the Lord put forth his hand and touched my mouth.

And the Lord said unto me, 'Behold, I have put my words in your mouth. See, I have this day sent thee over the nations and over the kingdoms to root out and to pull down, and to destroy, and to throw down, to build and plant."

After facing what Dathan and Korah faced, the Rastafarian squad could never be seen nor be heard again. It was only the others whom were in operation. These were not very much tough like those Rastafarians. However I remember one night to have perceived of another male entity that acted one way or the other like the previous headman.

He had a very groggy, strong and scaring voice. I will call him Spiker (not his real name).I perceived of him as a demon in a higher position.

All the others feared him so much such that when he

commanded; the rest trembled as they frowned to total quietness. As I perceived of him, he was like someone whom had great control over kingdoms and governments.He also boasted that he could destroy churches. He seemed to be someone who could devise anything evil and no one could stop him. Music was coming out from his strongholds as did the headman.

One could hear Bongo music; reggae music, Giriama local music, and gospel music come out freely from his evil strongholds.

Again and again, he commanded in a harsh and fierce voice,

"Come on, I want right now some people to go to Kokote's house, bind him hands and feet and drag him here."

In some of that music, I could hear them mention my name as they also prophesied about me, a fact that I didn't like. As I rebuked him and his evil strongholds, he started flying here and there restlessly.

Sometimes as I commanded them to go to hell, I could perceive of them as they went up to around the mouth of hell and got stuck there – Isaiah 5:14. Some minutes later, I could hear them plus their strongholds flying back. He stationed it somewhere and the threatening went on. Some evil strong holds and demons, when I rebuked them, I perceived of them go right away to hell.

I hated his voice very much as I told him;

"Listen, you Satan with your fellow demonic spirits plus your music strongholds, you have neither authority nor power over me. You are defeated in the mighty name of Jesus Christ."

There was something that amazed me very much about this creature. I could perceive of him, in between commands that he was always in deep sleep.

He just slept as Music came out freely from his evil stronghold. As this drama went on, my wife and I had already prayed and were lying on bed. We had also put off the lights.

As the command was passed on, I could truly see some weird figures dropping inside the room through the closed window. One after the other, they dropped inside as they held things that seemed to be like huge torches with red and thin lights. Those flashing gadgets were probably some submachine guns and the operators were the old man's soldiers- *askari wa mzee* as referred in chapter two.

I shook my wife as I said,

"Fiddlesticks, Loice! Loice! Get up and let's pray. You don't know what is happening right now .Come on, let's pray."

She retorted,

"Ah, we have already prayed by faith. Don't fear them lets sleep. You know I feel tired and sleepy."

And so, I jerked up with a start and rebuked them severely in Jesus' mighty name. Spiker was asleep as I could hear a Giriama local song coming out from his evil stronghold.

The music was saying,

"A servant of God can never be deceived. Kokote, I am the Lord your God. The devil is a liar and he is teasing you just for nothing. Don't fear him. Now look unto me and I will fight for you."

And so I wondered;

"Doesn't the devil hear these messages? Don't they come out from his music strongholds?"

Sometimes that music could pass bible messages like in the book of **Mark 13:9.**

That says,

"But take heed to yourselves: for they shall deliver you up to councils: and in the synagogues ye shall be beaten: and ye shall be brought before rulers and kings for my sake for a testimony against them."

CHAPTER 7

THE WHIP OF GOD

Although the devil is a defeated foe, he does not believe it, as shown through his persistent actions.

All this time, he kept on insisting that I should be sent to him so that I could be converted to devil worship. That beast thought that no one whatsoever the case could outwit him. I rebuked them on and on in Jesus' mighty name as I felt like someone being dragged towards that evil congregation.

Those messengers did whatever they could as at that time they feared for their lives. I felt surrounded as this being did all that he could and could not get to hurt me as I said;

"Satan, I don't belong to you. I belong to Jesus Christ of Nazareth and you are defeated in the mighty name of Jesus." As I said this, I was released.

I once heard those messengers saying;

"We thank the man of God that at least he presented himself before our leader. You know we would have been killed if he would have refused."

The devil knew that whenever he chose to come by himself he would be defeated. He is a great deceiver and so he always chooses to command other people rather than doing it himself.

All in all, I got total deliverance by the power of the Lord Jesus Christ as the word of God says,

"For the scripture says, whosoever believeth in Him shall not be ashamed. For there is no difference between the Jew and the Greek for the same Lord overall is rich unto all that call upon Him.

For whosoever shall call upon the name of the Lord shall be saved."

Rom: 10:11-13.

One day as I was outside our residence, Likoni-Mombasa, I heard some people walking as they talked. One of them said; *"surely Kokote is very powerful. As you go for him, you should make sure that you don't stay in the front line. He will just carry you off, over and out completely. He wouldn't care about whom you are."*

Another one answered, *"The man belongs to God. God loves him very much.*

Whenever he calls upon His name, He does things for him." One among them retorted; *"well then why can't; he ask Him to bless him with children and a job?"*

Someone else echoed; *"but still, if its children and a job, he will get but only if he*

keeps on praying."

There was a certain night whereby I was asleep by the side of my wife, suddenly; I was woken up in the course of the midnight perceiving of a clear presence of some sorcerers who had paid a visit. Two of them outside the window were a man and a woman, while far off, there was another one and a woman at that. They also perceived that I had fully woken up. The woman near the window called upon the other one far off, *"Salma! (Not her real name). Come and stand right here near the window. Jimmy! (Not his real name), just look at Salma. She is a coward. Salma don't you see that you are the one who is ailing? You are always going to the hospital for treatment. Who'll stand to lose, coward! Let's go."* They then quickly took off.

Those devil agents were always on a mission, commissioned by their leaders. One night, I had already prayed and was setting myself to go to sleep. I heard three sorcerers discussing about coming after me. Two were men while the third one was a woman. The woman told the men to opt her out of that mission as she said she was fearing to even come near me.

Isaiah 54:17 *"…..No weapon that is fashioned against you shall prosper, and you shall confute every tongue that rises against you in judgment."*

At times, I would just face them directly towards their direction and address them, *"listen you sorcerers, do all that you can do, but you will never prevail".* I would also pray through Isaiah 10:25-26, *"For in a very little while my indignation will come to an end and my anger will be directed to their destruction. And the Lord of hosts will wield against them a scourge……"*

I would then ask God to put this scourge/whip in my right hand and I would then tell them, *"Ok, listen you workers of iniquity! I raise this whip of God up and against your backs and heads in Jesus' mighty name"* and I repeated this for several times until I perceived that,

that meeting was disrupted and confused as everyone scattered to different directions while they cried sarcastically.

On the latter days, my wife and I would hear some wailings coming across through the night. Sometimes it could be from women, kids or men. It would happen as we were actually praying and rebuking those forces of darkness. I could hear what they might be saying while my wife could not. She could only hear the wailings or the commotion emanating from people outside whom were uncomfortable. She would only get what they said if ever she prayed to God and asked Him to reveal it to her. This would happen only by God's will.

There was once upon a time whereby my wife and I used to reside in Magongo –Mombasa. We rented a room whereby only we and the landlady were the occupants. I used to wake up early in the morning and at 5.00am went for work. In a period of some days, I started telling my wife that our landlady was a sorceress. She answered; ***"But I had known her for quite a long time, I think she is just o.k". I then told her; "Well, you are just ignorant but wait. Any day, maybe I might not be around. If you happen to hear her speaking in an unknown language to an unknown entity, then pray to God and*** *ask Him in Jesus' mighty name to let you perceive of what she is upto and God will let you know."*

It happened that one day; I woke up very early in the morning, prepared myself and went to work. Behind my back, something weird was happening about that sorceress. It was likely some few minutes past 5.00 am and my wife was fully awake. In the third room, that woman woke up and got out of her bed. She appeared to withdraw some oils out of her drawers, anointed herself and started talking to an unknown entity – a demonic spirit and in an unknown language with somehow a heavy tone.

Immediately, my wife went out slowly, stood outside that woman's room and listened. Unfortunately, she could not perceive of that language. She then asked Jesus; *"Jesus, my Lord and saviour, please! Let me know what this woman is talking about."*At once, the Lord Jesus let her hear what that woman was saying. That sorceress told that demonic spirit; *"you asked me to offer you my eldest daughter, but I begged you to spare her life and instead, I gave you her first born daughter. Although you consumed her, you were not pleased and so I gave you her newly born baby. You have also consumed that infant but now you insist that I give you their mother. Please, I beg you to let her live her* *life. You have also not yet let me get what I want".* Everyone knew about the death of those kids and so it downed to my wife with a force and she thought ; *"So they were offered as human sacrifice?"* when she had heard that weird communication, she immediately gathered some new energy for prayers. She went to our room, threw herself upon the bed and at once, she started praying the prayers by faith as in the book of Acts. When Paul and Silas prayed until the gates of the prison opened Acts 16:25-26.She prayed prayers without doubt James 1:5-8

"If any of you lacks wisdom, let him ask God, who gives to all men generously and without reproaching and it will be given him. But let him ask in faith without doubting, for he who doubts is like a wave of the sea that is driven and tossed by the wind. For that person must not suppose that a double –minded man, unstable in all his ways, will receive anything from the Lord."

Mathew 21:18-22 *"And Jesus answered them, 'Truly, I say to you, if you have faith and never doubt, you will not only do what has been done to this fig tree, but even if you say to this mountain, Be taken up and cast into the sea, it will be done. And whatever you ask in prayer, you will receive if you have faith."* Luke 11:5-9 *"And he said to them, 'which of you who has a friend will go to him at midnight and say to him, 'friend, lend me three loaves, for a friend of mine has arrived on a journey, and I have nothing to set before him; and he will answer from within, 'Do not bother me, the door is now shut, and my children are with me in bed, I cannot get up and give you anything. I tell you, though he will not get up and give him anything because he is his friend, yet because of his importunity he will rise and give him whatever he needs. And I tell you, ask and it will be given to you; seek, and you will find; knock, and it be open to you."*

Hebrews 10:38; the word of God says, *"But my righteous one shall live by faith and if he shrinks back, my soul has no pleasure in him."*

Dear reader, it's dangerous to pray without faith. Whenever one prays and later on shrinks back, because he sees God tarring, the devil is right there and mind you, he is using the same book Hebrews 10:38. He says; *"See this person, he is mine because he lacks faith."* I don't guess in this, I know it is how he acts. So make haste my friend and do things wisely in the way of God.

You don't have to wait for God to grant you a foreign language for you to be able to pray. Just pray by faith and God is there to give you help. Sometimes God chooses to use some hard lessons to make someone to be a prayerful warrior as in Daniel 3:1-. These days by God's grace, I can easily see those people who intermingle in the powers of darkness. I often but not always see those people communicating into the dark world. It doesn't matter whether they have their mouth shut or not. Even if they are talking a different topic, still I can see them tapping into the dark kingdom. All this is done through God's intervention.

There was once another day, during my first days of this battle, when my wife and I were sitting outside our home. Far beyond, ten houses and about a blind corner, I could hear someone talking just to himself. It appeared to be what was transpiring in his mind. It didn't matter how far but what he was thinking was coming through and directly towards me. I told my wife; ***"Now, look towards this direction, there is a man who will appear heading in our direction. Just look at him and I will ask you something."***

This was what he said, *"let me go and pass by the side of the servant of God. He is right now sitting outside his home. I just wish to have a look at him."*

There, he appeared and as he passed by, we could have a good look at him. He was a Rastafarian and having a brown tinted skin. I asked my wife, *"What do you have to say about him?"*

"I think he is just a normal person." She answered. *"No way, he is just a devil."* I told her.

One gruesome night, I had just come back from work. I was still residing in Likoni-Mombasa. I had just finished praying and outside the house, I could hear some commotion. My wife could perceive of it also. She told me, *"I can hear some commotion emanating from outside. They appear to be people who are furious about something. They seem to walk here and there as they murmur audibly in the darkness"* I was hearing all that they were saying and planning in the darkness. *"That's the spirit of terrorism"* I said. *"Let's kneel down and pray. Let's break that stronghold of the devil in Jesus' name."*

As we did pray, I could hear them people, a huge congregation gathering in a temple. They were men, women and children among whom I could perceive of the presence of some sorcerers and witchdoctors masquerading as their leaders. Among them, there were the ones that mainly acted as soldiers. They were referred by the others, *'The old man's soldiers (askari wa mzee)."* Those soldiers were the ones whom were always commanded;

"Come on, you two go bring so and so alive."

Here is where I say if you don't have the authority and the power of Jesus Christ of Nazareth in you, then you are stuck there filling buckets with urine or running away in fear. It's like when Jesus' disciples took to their heels as their master was arrested. Prior to this, He warned them, *"Watch and pray so that you may not come to temptation."*

They thought that sleep was better for their health and so they chose it for the worst. If you are not born again and not covered by the blood of Jesus, then those powers of darkness might also manifest for the worst. Most people die temporarily as they are taken captive by those dark forces. Relatives and friends might go for the burial services, but it might only be a trick. That deceased person could have been taken captive by the dark forces ready for human sacrifice.

It's only the people in Christ Jesus that are lucky and safe. Revelation 14:13 says, ***"blessed are the people who die in the Lord as from now...."*** Ref: Psalms 116:15. Back to the previous story, I could hear one of their leaders broadcasting to them; ***"Alright! Alright! All women to sit down on this side while all the men to sit on the other side. All of you children, come on, sit here in front."***

On the pulpit in front, there was the whole lot of sorcerers putting their sorcery stronghold in place.

As I perceived of it, there were also some guest sorcerers and witchdoctors among them. I had also known that different groups of the kids would be getting in front to sing and praise their god whom I perceived to be Satan. The attendants were people from different parts of the country-Kenya. One group after the other, sang their songs of worship as they hit their tumplines, and blew their flutes while they danced. All of this, I could perceive in the spiritual realm whether I prayed or didn't. On the pulpit, their leaders were around five to seven. As the praises went on, that satanic presence was expected to grow stronger and stronger. I could also perceive that, the whole aim of them doing so was to start a counter-religion warfare between different faiths. That was being planned through witchcraft from the dark side of the world. I had come to know that most things, before they manifest physically, they are planned previously in the spiritual realm.

CHAPTER 8

HUMAN SACRIFICE

My wife and I were onto our knees praying. She could also hear them as they sang, but could not be able to interpret what transpired in the spiritual realm. All of that was done for one goal, to start some counter religion violence throughout the country and the whole world, but one thing was the obstacle.

"Kokote is the stumbling block. (The Holy Spirit of God is actually the restraining force-2 Thess.2:3-12). He is harassing us with his prayers. Every time he prays, he destroys our plans and actually kills some of us. Whenever we conduct our meetings, he is just being informed. One can say nothing about him without him knowing. One thing, Kokote should be killed and be put out of the way, but how?

He is actually dangerous. When he sleeps, you don't see him completely and sometimes, you just see battalions of angels surrounding the whole place. He is always protected by his God and a Pokomo at that. Are all Pokomos like this? If they are, then they must be totally cut off this world." One among them added;

"The man is really loved by his God. Besides worshipping Him, he sometimes just talks to Him and He does things for him. We are actually confused. How really does Kokote worship God?"

The songs were being sang on and on in the darkness. My wife and I were onto our knees praying. One of their leaders was at the stronghold. He had started reading some witchcraft verses from his sorcery book. He was actually shooting some sorcery missiles towards our direction. I stopped praying, faced towards their direction and addressed them, *"listen! Satan and your fellow demonic spirits plus all of you workers of iniquity/devil agents. You will not prevail in this in Jesus' mighty name. You are all under arrest in Jesus' mighty name. I command that satanic stronghold to erupt in flames in Jesus' mighty name."*

Immediately, I perceived of that satanic stronghold erupting in flames. All of those witchcraft operators were dramatically hurled up and around in flames. As they were moving around and around in the sky burning, they were crying sarcastically saying, *"Let the God that Kokote worships give him the job that he is asking for and the children that he wants. We are tired of being tormented by his prayers."*

They were wailing and wailing while they were up and around burning. All the rest were looking on confused. During the whole of that time, they were asking, **"How does Kokote worship God and how do the others do it?"**

I thought, "Maybe, they have really repented and God has now released all of my blessings. They were the real dark forces that had been blocking my blessings but now, glory to God."

They were up in torment for about a half an hour and I thought, **"At least, things are over,"** But alas! After that, they were released and they were raging with anger-hurling threats and insults at me.

"Kokote will never get that job he is asking for. Maybe he gets a job in farting. He will also not get any children with his wife."

I addressed them, **"well, you have not yet repented? Still you will not prevail in this. Be defeated in the mighty name of Jesus."** I thought, **"Okay another time will come, even if they seem to be repentant,**

I will not relent. I will keep fighting them while they are up and around in torment- in Jesus' mighty name."

Most of the time, when there is a disco, a burial or a wedding ceremony somewhere and there is some evil powers behind, I could just perceive of it. I would then start rebuking that evil stronghold in Jesus' mighty name. When it flies off, I could just perceive of the remaining congregation to comprise of normal men, women and or with children. In most of those gatherings, if they could be wanting to sacrifice a child or a person, I just say, ***"Hey! You workers of iniquity. You will not prevail in this. That person will not be sacrificed. I cover them with the blood of Jesus. They belong to Jesus Christ of Nazareth."*** Psalms 14:4

They could not be able to touch them. Sometimes, I would sleep and when I woke up, I could hear them say, ***"Hey! What do we do with this child? And what about her mother?"*** I would say, ***"Listen to me you iniquity workers, that man/child belongs to God. Jesus knows what he will do with them. But as for you, I rebuke you in Jesus' mighty name."***

There was once upon a time while my wife and I were residing in Kisumu ndogo-Malindi. We happened to be inside our rented room while far at the new market, I could hear some music played on.

Behind the curtains, I could perceive of some evil/dark operations going on around that music stronghold. I thought, ***"well, I will go there to the new market and***

take a stroll.''

As I arrived there, just on the side of the road, there were those modern herbalists, two of them advertising their herbal medicines. They were two of them whom appeared to be smart in their nice suits. They had also placed there some music system with two huge speakers just playing music to woe those people watching to buy their medicines. I went there and watched for some few seconds and as I turned to go, I perceived of something weird happening behind me. I had just gone around five metres away from that place. As I turned again to look at them, I became totally amazed. Those two herbalists had automatically turned to be two native doctors. From their waists upward, they were clearly naked, painted and holding some cow tails/whisks. They were doing that stuff that witch doctors normally do when they have customers. As I went near, they changed into those smart guys in suits. When I chose to go, they turned to be native doctors. Dear reader, you might happen to be in a bar, a burial or a wedding ceremony or in any social gathering. It's never bad but its wisdom that you always have to check yourself and counter check your stand in the things of God. Are you salvation wise ok? Are you covered by the blood of Jesus Christ? You might be attending a social gathering which might only be the devils hoax. You might be there while at the same time happen to be in the sea attending a devils meeting or also happen to be in front of a native doctor. God is total love and it's always good for one to choose to live within His mighty love. In John 3:16-18 the word of God says, ***"For God so loved the world that He gave His only son, that whoever believes in Him should not perish, but have eternal life. For God sent the son into the world, not to condemn the world, but that the world might be saved through Him. He who believes in Him is not condemned, he who does not believe is condemned already, because he has not believed in the name of the only son of God."***

CHAPTER 9

<u>SATAN'S WARFARE TACTICS</u>

The bible 2Cor 2: 10-11 tells us not to be ignorant of Satan's tactics-ref. Eph 5:7-14. The word of God also says that the devil is our adversary 1 Pet.5:6-11 who prowls here and there roaring like a lion seeking for someone to devour. The devil is never a lion, but if God only lets you get a glimpse of this beast and see how he prowls and roars, I think you would be running a hundred meters race towards Jesus Christ just to ask for God's mercy.

Another quick option that you will habour in mind is for you to hide inside your wardrobe and leave a free space just enough for your nose. Thanks for the word of God Matt.11:28 which says; ***"Come to me all of you who work and are heavy ladden and I will give you rest".*** It is only when you truly take note of your enemy's moves that you will be able to wage war against him. Here, I will illustrate a few tactics that he usually likes using while he wages war against people and especially the saints.

(a) The first tactic is that, the enemy strikes some evil missiles to people in most cases while they are asleep Matt 13:24-25. In the book of Matt 26:40-4; Jesus Christ asked His disciples; ***"so, could you not***

watch with me one hour? Watch and pray that you may not enter into temptations". Satan strikes bad omen into people's hearts, especially to the saints while they are asleep. He is mainly concerned with the saints because he knows that he cannot get them while they are alert. Immediately you wake up from sleep, alas! The enemy has already stricken and he is also near you but most vulnerable.

As you wake up, he is on the run and so you don't wait until you sober up.

You just arrest him in his evil truck and ask him to carry all his burdens and be cast off to hell in Jesus' mighty name. These weeds/ curses that the devil sows in people's hearts will always have specific names. They will always be curses like; sickness, poverty, divorce, barrenness and etc.

Even if you don't perceive of them in the spirit, you just pray as you mention them by faith and cast them off to hell in Jesus' mighty name. If you will wait so as to sober up from sleep, you will find that he has already gone far and has also gained the best grip against you.

The devil is just a spirit that is, even if you whisper, he just hears. However, circumstances will always tell whether you will use less or more force in dealing with the enemy.

All in all, the word of God reminds us that the war is not ours but it belongs to the Lord. This devil's tactic also goes hand in hand with bad dreams. Most bad dreams come from the devil. These maybe dreams about weird animals chasing after you, about walking outside your house in the middle of the night and sometimes naked. They may be dreams about committing sexual intercourse outside wedlock, about fornication, about other people having sex, about yourself smoking cigarettes or taking alcohol.

One may also see himself or other people swimming in a river or in the sea and it might also be about eating food in one's dreams. For the born again brethren, it's only through prayers that you will be able to break the evil mess that comes along with such evil dreams. You will definitely have to resist the devil with his evil dreams and cast him off to hell in Jesus Christ's mighty name. But for my fellow friends who are off the salvation line, I say take care and sober up. The devil is never a joker while hell is never about fresh and cold water but real unquenchable fire Mark 9:43. The word of God says; *"Son of man, speak to the sons of your people and say to them, suppose that I bring a sword upon a land, and all the people of that land take a man and make him their watchman, and he sees a sword coming upon the land and blows the horn and warns the people. If someone hears the sound of the horn but does not heed the warning and a sword comes and takes his life, his blood will be on his own head. He heard the sound of the horn, but he did not heed the warning. His blood will be upon himself. If he had heed the warning, his life would have been saved."* Ezekiel 33:1-5.

b) The second means that the devil uses in attacking people is by soothsaying. He can decorate you with a lot of Godly tittles but alas! Behind the scene, he is devising some new ways of attack. In the book of Acts 16:16-18 the word of God says; *"as we were going to the place of prayer, we were met by a slave girl who had a spirit of divination and brought her owners much gain by sooth saying. She followed Paul and us crying, 'these men are servants of the most high God who proclaim to you the way of salvation. And this she did for many days. But Paul was annoyed, and turned and said to the spirit, 'I charge you in the name of Jesus Christ to come out of her. And it came out that very hour."* Paul had come to his senses that that evil spirit was actually devising some evil ways behind the curtain to attack them.

It's never just a beautiful scene to always have the devil behind you in appraisal. It's actually disgusting as the devil does not relent so much quickly. Sometimes he might start acting as a switched on robot. He can easily frustrate you if you don't switch him off at once.

(c)The enemy may also strike through horrible arguments and negative thinking. In 2 Cor .10:3-6 the word of God says; *"For though we live in the world, we are not carrying on worldly war, for the weapons of our war fare are not worldly but have divine power to destroy strongholds. We destroy arguments and every proud obstacle to the knowledge of God and take every thought captive to obey Christ, being ready to punish every disobedience, when your obedience is complete."*

Here, the battle simply starts from the mind. Negative thinking always comes from the devil. One might start thinking; "Oh so and so, I will never forgive just because he has beaten up my child". Or else one might think; 'my wife is so much nagging and so I think I shall have to divorce her." All such thoughts and much more negative ones come to people directly from the devil. Immediately such thoughts come into your mind, you can simply rebuke them in Jesus Christ's mighty name. One should address such a negative thought this way; *"you evil thought! You don't come from God; neither you don't belong to me. Come out of me you demon and be cast off to hell in Jesus Christ's mighty name."* The word of God tells us to take every thought captive to obey Christ. One day, God made it clear to me that, negative thinking is harmful to people and also a manipulation from the devil. I was unto my knees praying, struggling out in a spiritual war fare. Suddenly I perceived of the top of my head open. What I got from that was just terrible. It was like drums and drums of evil sentences being poured into my head. Those were statements like;

"I will kill you stupid, "you will be crazy and you will divorce." Those and much more evil statements were downloading into my head. It was a downpour of negative statements. That day I spent a sleepless and horrible night. As hard as I rebuked off those evil statements, they kept pouring like hell. Later on, that ordeal was cut off completely. This just means that God doesn't want people to be passive neither in their minds nor in their deeds. When you don't use your mind (just dormant) or don't use it for positive thinking, the devil takes it over for his own evil agenda. In Ecc.7:21-22,the word of God says; *"Do not give heed to all of the things that men say, lest you hear your servant cursing you; your heart knows*

that many times you have yourself cursed others..."

Here is where evil arguments come in. This is also when you see someone actually take the position of a donkey. A donkey may stand in one position while it only uses its ears to gather information coming from all directions. This only shows that you are idle and so just do it and you will find your neighbors speaking evil of you. If you don't realize that it's only demonic and go unto your knees and destroy such arguments through prayers, the devil will build an evil stronghold against you.

This is very simple that immediately you see your neighbors congregate outside your house and talking evil about you-backstabbing you, just cut off their evil arguments through prayers. By doing so, you just find that everything comes back to normal and all of them maintain positive conversation .They all become good neighbors. Here is where you find Jesus upon the cross saying; ***"Father, forgive them for they do not know what they are doing."***Mathew27:21-23.The bible tells us to destroy evil arguments just by the power of prayers.

There was once upon a time whereby I slept and as I woke up, I could perceive of three evil entities-two men and a woman. I could perceive of one of them to be Satan. The woman, I can only guess that she was the queen of the sea. I could perceive of all of them to be evil spirits. As I woke up, I could note that they were engaged in an evil conversation against me. I just addressed them; ***"You demonic spirits, I bind you in Jesus Christ's mighty name. Every tongue that you raise against me and my wife, I bring down unto judgment in Jesus mighty name. All evil weapons that you are fashioning against us let them be destroyed just because of us. That evil argument of yours, I bring down unto destruction in Jesus' mighty name"***. As this was done, they quickly disappeared into the thin air, Isaiah 54:11-17.The word of God also says; ***"or how can one enter a strong man's house and plunder his goods, unless he first binds the strong man? Then indeed he may plunder his house-Mathew 12:29"*** If you don't pray and bind evil spirits freely, hovering around you, then you will never quit leaving in bondages.

d) The forth tactic that the enemy uses is through multiple attacking angles. In the book of numbers 23; 24 the word of God is talking about the different angles that the enemy uses while he attacks. In most cases, the enemy uses around three or more angles. Here in the book of numbers, the word of God is talking about Balaam the prophet and Balak the king of Moab and the three different angles they used so as to attack the Israelites. In Mathew4: 1-11, the word of God is also talking about three positions that Satan /the tempter used in attacking Jesus.

It also seems that he uses some percentages in his attack against people. I had experienced it in several times in my life as he attacked.

 As he strikes, he would come with an evil force of around 100 percent. As I rebuked him in Jesus' mighty name, he would go and come back from another angle with around 50 percent evil force. He doesn't relent so much easily, because he used to come the third time in another angle with about 20 percent evil power.

As I rebuked him for the third time, he would quit and so I retained the Lord Jesus' peace and coolness.

 (e)The fifth tactic that he uses is through false religions. In Timothy 4:1,-5, the word of God says,

"Now the Spirit expressly says that in latter days, some will depart from the faith by giving heed to deceitful spirits and doctrines of demons, through the

pretentions of liars whose consciences are seared, who forbid marriage and enjoin abstinence from foods which God created to be received with thanks giving by those who believe and know the truth." I have seen the devil manifesting in some few churches and in some of other religions. Remember! Satan proclaims himself to be god but alas! He is just an imposter Ezekiel 28. One day, as my wife and I were just resting in our bed, we could perceive of a neighboring church conducting an overnight drive (kesha). We could both hear them singing choruses, preaching and praying. Just behind the curtain, I could perceive of Satan, manifesting behind their leader /soloist. The others singing with him had also turned out to be real devils. I could hear some evil operations going on about that squad. Immediately I perceived of this, I started praying until I perceived of that evil strong hold peeling off that congregation and started to fly. . I rebuked it off until it went to hell and left that squad just as normal people. I did this for around three weeks time on Fridays, and later on, I heard of a tragic thing that happened to that church and I wondered as to why? Did they really involve themselves in weird dealings? I could find this happening in two to three churches. I also noted it happen in some other two religions and in some notable numbers of social gatherings .

Whenever I prayed, I could find those evil strongholds flying off and leaving those congregations to comprise of just normal people. The bible gives us a precise way of checking and noting whether a church is on the right course or not. In 2 John 7-11, the word of God says; ***"For many deceivers have gone out into the world, men who will not acknowledge the coming of Jesus Christ in the flesh; such a one is the deceiver and the antichrist. Look to yourselves, that you may not loose what you have worked for, but may win a full reward. Anyone who goes ahead and does not abide in the doctrine of Christ does not have God. He who abides in the doctrine has both the father and the son .If anyone comes to you and does not bring this doctrine, do not receive him into the house or give him any greetings; for he who greets him shares his wicked work."*** The true gospel is the one about the death and the resurrection of Jesus Christ as also noted in Galatians 1:8-9. The obligation to preach the gospel of Christ is laid upon all believers without any exception Mark 16; 15-18.

There was once upon a time whereby I was attending a certain church. The gospel of Jesus Christ was preached within that church but there were some alterations here and there about the word of God. Once, I went there and found people and infants being baptized with some water from a container/a bowl. I then thought, ***"This, I haven't seen it anywhere within the word of God."*** I therefore went and found another good church somewhere else. There are churches that preach about the gospel of the heavenly Father, but are they authorized by the word of God? John 4: 1-6. Others preach about the gospel of washing of feet while others preach about specific days of worship. The bible tells us that all days are good for worship and no one should corn anyone in this – Colossians 2:16 -19 and Romans 14:5-8. The question is this: ***"Is it the gospel of Jesus Christ that brings about salvation?"*** Heb 2: 3, the word of God asks us; ***"How shall we escape if we neglect such a great salvation?"*** The Devil is very much cunning. He has a lot of fake churches and manmade religions just to keep people out of God's grace. There is also a sure way to check and know that God is surely present and alive. Dear reader, if you know that you are surely born again, start preaching/testifying about the death and resurrection of Jesus Christ and about salvation. As you go on ministering to people, also note the ones that are actually bound directly by the devil/demonically possessed. If you are really involved in dealing deliverance prayers on them, not so long, you will have stepped on a live wire in the devil's kingdom. As he is confused, he will start trying to strike back in one way or the other. Mind you the devil is always serious and so you have always to concentrate upon the cross where by Jesus was crucified. Be soapy and you will end up being the devil's breakfast – Psalm 14:4.

As soon as Satan comes into the scene, Jesus Christ is also right there beside you. Ask God for anything pertaining that spiritual war fare in Jesus' mighty name and He will do it for you. All in all dear brethren, our Lord Jesus told us that immediately one notices that there is a spec in his brother's eye, he should first of all sit down and pluck out that whole log that is inside his own eye, Mathew.7:3-5. It is then he shall see clearly and be able to pluck out that spec in his brother's eye. Jesus Christ gave us authority Mark16:16 but alas!One should use this authority to first of all deal with that whole horde of demons/curses within himself. This authority surely works that way.

(f)   The last but not the least of those tactics of the devil that he uses in warfare is through doorways. Alot of things can be the door ways used by demonic spirits to attack people. That is why immediately one gets saved; he is needed to do some total overhaul repentance about his past life. It would also be a nice thing if you note down on a piece of paper every committed sin that you probably know of. If you are a man, how many women did you ever fornicate with? If you are a woman, how many men did you ever commit sin with whether outside marriage or before salvation? How many witchdoctors have you ever encountered with and you probably know them? Lev. 19:31 and Lev.20:6.

i. Are you a drug addict or a drunkard? Gal. 5: 19-21.

ii. Do you actually attend disco? Gal.5:19-21.

iii. Were you a sorcerer before being born again? Gal.5:19-21.

iv. Do you convey fits of anger?

v. Are you hostile?

vi. Are you a liar? Rev.21:7-8 and John 8:44.

vii. Are you mean?

viii. Were you a lesbian, a homosexual or a sodomite before you got saved? Rom.1.24-32.

ix. Have you ever committed murder? Rev.21:7-8 and 1 John 3:15-18.

x. Have you ever committed an abortion? Rev .21:7-8.

xi. Are you a murmurer or a slanderer? 1 cor.10:10. And Matt. 15:19.

xii. Are you quarrelsome?: Gal.5:19-21

xiii. Have you ever involved yourself in masturbation?
   Gen 38:8-10.

The list can actually be so big. About those past sins, it's surely —advisable that one should lock himself inside his room and repent of all of them one, by one before God and ask for forgiveness. It's also better if someone fasts as he does this. Lastly, one has to remember to rebuke all demonic spirits that had infested him from one issue to the others. Demonic spirits can really be moved by the command of born again people who are really fasting and praying. Demons are spirits so you may command them in a low voice or loudly and they just hear. There was once upon a time where by I was fasting and praying for just three days on half day basis.

To my amazement, as I prayed and commanded those evil forces, they were being turned here and there as one opens the pages of a book. I said; ***"My Lord Jesus, are they puppets?"***

Always remember! Unrepented sins will always be used as door ways for demonic spirits to come and attack. There are also some other things that people undergo in life which are actually their past deeds harvest. In Galatians 6:7-8, the word of God says; ***"Do not be deceived; God is not mocked for whatever a man sows, that he will*** *also reap. For he who sows to his own flesh will from the flesh reap corruption; but he who sows to the spirit will from the spirit reap eternal life."* This verse does not offer any exception. It does not matter whether a person is born again or not. Immediately a person is born again, God automatically gives them a short duration of peace and coolness. It's better for all people to use this short duration for learning about the will of God. One can surely learn the will of God by reading the word of God and also by attending new believer's classes. The reason as to why one should be quick in learning God's will is because God will soon; though for a short duration leave you to reap what you had really sown. Were you a drug addict? An adulterer? A frequent visitor to witchdoctors? The list is quite long and so He just let you pass through a desert whereby you just grope in the darkness wondering whether God is really present. Of course God is there right at your side .He also lets you pass through this just to see how much you have grown up in faith.

This is also Gods plan to let you reap what you have really sown .Remember just call Him whenever you see an obstacle in your life and He is very much swift to make you pass over that obstacle .This goes on for quite a short duration and thereafter, you just see yourself stable and upright in your salvation .In that short duration He just comes in and deliver you from every hard situation you had been encountering. After all this, God is very much pleased and honored about your maturity in your salvation.

God is never a tempter, but its Satan who is so and as he goes to God to ask for permission to tempt people, God is in most occasions obligated to let him.

God does it only to take note about those tempted whether they will continue standing upright in their faith believing in Him or not.

James 1:13-15, the word of God says this; *"Let no one say, when he is tempted; 'I am tempted by God? For God cannot be tempted with evil and He Himself temps no one but each person is tempted when he is lured and enticed by his own desire. Then desire when it has conceived gives birth to sin, and sin when it is full grown brings forth death."* The word of God tells us that there is now no more condemnation for those who are in Christ Jesus Roman 8:1.

While this is true, however about reaping what one sows still, it's the same word of God.

<u>NB:</u> *It's also advisable that when you pray, you enlist* *at least a prayer item for about three and above issues. You will be doing it at least in every twenty four hours. Satan is always on the run to seal one item after the other/ one at a time. Every time he tries to seal one item, the others are leaking and at last, he is completely shattered off.*

CHAPTER 10:

<u>THE DESTROYER</u>

As I went on praying, I could actually feel the forces of darkness pinning me onto the wall shown by the fact that I didn't have children, a job, and a house nor had I any wealth. There was a time whereby, I came face to face with the destroyer as written in the book of John 10:10. ***"The thief comes only to steal and kill and destroy; I came that they may have life and have it abundantly."***

My wife and I would have already prayed and just resting on our bed. It seems that prayers are always established in the spiritual realm heading straight towards God.

This happens especially when one prays in spirit and truth by faith and without doubt - James 1:5-8. Three to five minutes later, I could perceive of some spirit entities in the sky that appeared to be so much elated. They said; ***"Hey guys give respect, God Himself is blessing Kokote with money"***- Isaiah 33:1. And they went on counting – two million, 5 million, 12 million and immediately with the speed of lightening, the destroyer appeared and started stealing. All those spirit entities in the air could start shouting at once; ***"Oh, thief, thief, Satan is a thief; he is stealing Kokote's money".***

Something else also happened to me while I was very young and a standard four pupil in Kiunga –Lamu.

It was lunch time and I was just walking along the road towards home for lunch. Just abruptly, in the middle of the road, I found a large pile of money like a huge mound containing pure notes. I bent forward and picked a note, and it was a hundred shillings note in my hand. What about the rest? They quickly vanished. At that time, I even didn't know about salvation nor vision. I went home and informed my sister - sister Grace. I gave her the note, she bought some sugar and other food stuff, we feasted and I forgot about that whole issue.

Joel 2:25. **"I will restore to you the years which the swarming locust has eaten, the hopper, the destroyer and the cutter, my great army which I sent among you."** That beast was extraordinarily violent. Other times as I prayed, I could actually find my words being established in the spiritual realm. I could see them forming a line, one word after the other, proceeding directly from my mouth heading up in the sky.

Some few minutes later, I could see the destroyer emerge like the flash of lightning and started eating my words one after the other-violently. Daniel 10:12-14 says; **"Then he** *said to me, 'Fear not, Daniel, for from the first day that you set your mind to understand and humbled yourself before your God, your words have been heard, and I have come because of your words.*

The prince of the kingdom of Persia withstood me twenty one days; but Michael, one of the chief princes, came to help me, so I left him there with the prince of the kingdom of Persia and came to make you understand what is to befall your people in the latter days for the vision is for days yet to come."

I would then start talking to my master and I said, *"Jesus Christ, my Lord and Saviour, what is this that I am seeing? See what the devil is doing. He is eating into my words (prayers). He has started feeding upon my line of prayers right from above (in the sky), shooting down towards me. Jesus, my master! What will he do next?"*

But alas! As the devil had finished feeding upon my line of prayers, he had already soared down and stood on the ground, directly facing me. He was mad at me, furious and full of insults. All in all, he could not be able to harm me in any way for I was divinely protected by God Himself. I would then start thinking;

"Dear Jesus, he has already eaten up my prayers. What do I do?" I would then offer another line of prayers to my God in Jesus' mighty name and the destroyer appeared and did the same thing. Later on, I started putting/laying some stumbling blocks along the line of prayers. I did it once, twice and thrice and the devil manifested onto the ground. He appeared to be the head of them all and he was raging with fury. He is a true terrorist. Surely, he is the father of terrorism. Among the rest, he was feared the most.

He said this;

"Kokote underestimates my powers and I will show him. I will send him back to school. I will check and find out what he likes the most. Whether it's money, a job, a house, children, women or whatever.

I shall have to catch him through either of them. He must not live, he must die and I will surely eat him up." I would then tell him;

"Listen to me you Satan, the word of God says this; 'whoever takes my blood and eats my flesh will never perish John 6:47-59.' My wife and I have already eaten the flesh and blood of Jesus Christ. We shall never die. We shall live to experience

God's blessings upon our lives."

My dear friend/reader, the devil is never a joker. Although he succeeded to convince one third of the angels of God in heaven to be on his side but then he was fought by Michael and his angels and was hurled down unto earth. He has no more place in heaven and has no more time left that is why he has gone into the world to fight those who keep the commandments of God and bear testimony to Jesus. Revelation 12:7- He knows that those people who are faithful to Jesus and bear the testimony to Him are the ones heading to heaven. He is full of jealousy and hatred towards this clique of people and so he had made a manifesto. In his manifesto, no any person should go to heaven. He feels that as he is banished off that place/heaven and doomed to roast in the lake of fire in hell, all people should be tormented together with him in that great furnace -Revelation 14:9-11.

During the whole of this spiritual warfare, I always used hit and defense mechanism. Sometimes when I found that the commotion was great, I used some over haul mechanism (God's weapon) and the outcome was great. Sometimes I actually commanded them to congregate in one place (battle field) which they did. As it happened, I sought for God's intervention. I would then say, *"Dear*

Jesus, the word of God says that the war does not belong to man-1 Samuel 17:47. Jesus, my Lord, take them on by the sword that comes out through your mouth Rev 19:15." After such a heavy spiritual warfare, everyone would be panting for breath and confused. They would say, *"Kokote has outdone us completely. What shall we do?"* One of them said, *"Hey, hey see this he has really killed some devils and people."* A man said; *"He has God's warrant to kill. We should not play around with him, let him alone."* A woman shouted, *"He has killed my two sons. How will I get them back? Bullshit, he must surely die."* Most of the time, I could actually hear them shouting bad words at me like, *"you will die, you will be sick, you will divorce, you will be barren."* And so I started nullifying whatever they said and their words were immediately cancelled off in the spiritual realm. Dear reader, this is only done in faith. For someone whom doesn't hear or see, his faith should be much greater than the faith of the one who discerns. If you just understand me, I mean it's when you appear as though you are blindfolded and you utter words of command (prayer) in faith. Things happen more quickly than the words of the seer. Still, for both of them, the same measure of faith is required.

CHAPTER 11

<u>IN THE PRESENCE OF THE MASTER-JESUS CHRIST.</u>

In one of those tiresome nights that I spent in the battle field fighting that spiritual warfare, something peculiar/unique happened. I could perceive of the devil and his evil battalion, insulting, cursing, setting and shooting their fiery darts at me. Here I reminded Jesus about what the word of God says in Matthew 11:28. *"Come to me, all of you who labour and are heavy laden, and I will give you rest."* I said, *"Jesus! This devil and his evil battalion have become a heavy burden upon my shoulders. Make me rest from that burden. Now, you devils are needed by Jesus Christ upon the cross. Off to the cross in Jesus' mighty name."* To my amazement, Satan and those two wizards were immediately hurled up into the presence of Jesus. There, Jesus appeared to be in an office having sat on a chair/throne. He started asking the devil some questions and I appeared to be there in the spirit; and Jesus asked;

"Satan! Why have you been oppressing Kokote for this long? Why do you oppress him for the things that are his? Why do you place a barrier before him?" He answered; *"because I have given him some work to do*

and he doesn't want to do it. I even sent him a present- a child/pregnancy and he said that the things of God are Satan's." By the way, like in the case of Job, you just don't know whether he will be told to; " ***Go and break his neck but let him alive.***" For a person to be present in such a scene to plead for mercy, it's only by God's will and grace- Job 2: 1-10. Jesus said; ***"Okay, you! Satan may now go and leave off your oppression. Leave Kokote alone."*** The devil is exceedingly arrogant and proud. He thinks that if he is given another chance, he would definitely kick Jesus out of the way and become more powerful instead. Such a scene is not so much pleasing to behold. You can be sure that the devil is not a joker. The devil was actually begging for a chance to have me so that he could kill me. I said; ***"Jesus, I am yours and I never know as to why the devil is after me. Dear Jesus, don't ever let my feet be removed from the boundary of your love. May your love abound upon me my master Jesus Christ."***

All through that period, there was something else- sinister happening. There was total commotion in the sky. There were a lot of satanic spirits flying up and down upon the earth. This one said this and another one said something else.

I started thinking of that situation whereby the devil

manifested in Peter and Jesus kicked him off. He said; *"Get behind me Satan for you are a hindrance to me."* Matt 16:23.

I thought, *"Well, it will become the devil if only Jesus gives him a very hard kick and tumbles him to hell."* I woke up my wife and told her to stay alert so that we could pray. I told her that there was an unusual thing happening in the spiritual realm. She woke up with a forceful start, quarrelling as though she were an angry buffalo woken up from sleep. I said; *"hey baby, don't shake off your sleep, get down to sleep. I will go on with prayers but know that some of these things concern you also."*

The devil was still stuck there and he said, *"Oh, leave Kokote to me. I have something special for him. Of course, he is not able to do God's calling."* Jesus answered, *"God will enable him. now go".*

A voice said, *"The pregnancy belongs to Kokote."* *"Oh no, I can see that you are depriving me of my vision. If this should happen like this, then let me get his wife."* He begged.

Jesus answered; *"Even the woman also has God's calling, you should let her alone. You may reach out into the world and find someone else to offer your* *vision. **Go now and let Kokote alone so that he may get all that belongs to him.*** *"* With that, I got to sleep and woke up early in the following Sunday morning. Satan had

come back on earth threatening to topple me over and eat me up as he put it. He was saying that I was given a pastoral job and I could not do it and that he had also given me a job and I refused to do it. What he was told to do was different from what he wanted to push down my throat. I could hear what he was saying behind the curtains. He said; ***"well, I will give him a job and if he accepts, I will have gotten him. I will kill and eat him straight away."*** I always reminded him that it's the work of the Holy Spirit to give out gifts but not the devil. And so I said; ***"You devil, may Jesus rebuke you!"*** 1Corinthians 12:4-11.When God promised to bless Abraham, he (Abraham) slaughtered some offerings Genesis 15:7-11 and put it before God to consume. God took some time/tarried to descend and so Abraham stayed there in the open, thwarting away vultures-demons. Later in the afternoon while Abraham was overwhelmed with some heavy sleep, God came and blessed him. About such hindrances you can read. Genesis: 7-11 and Daniel 10:12.There is a special time whereby the devil goes to heaven in the presence of God to ask for a chance to tempt all upright born again brethren. He begs God to give him such a chance. He tells God; ***"Well you say, such and such a person is yours but now, only give me a chance to go for him and you will see −a hypocrite".***

God accepts because He would want to feel good about those people that would stand by His side without wavering like in the case of Jesus - Luke 4:1-13; In the case of Peter- Luke 22: 31-32 says; ***"Simon, Simon, behold, Satan demanded to have you, that he might sift you like wheat, but I have prayed for you that your faith may not fail; and when you have turned again, strengthen your brethren."*** There is also the case of Daniel 3:8- and Job 1:1-12.

On that Sunday morning, my wife was preparing breakfast while I had gone out to brush my teeth.

As I did this, a sorceress manifested in front of me. She had two bouncers/ hit men on both sides. What I remember is that she was trying to do something evil against me. I rebuked her in the mighty name of Jesus Christ and they vanished at once as she let out a very loud shriek. As I got back inside the house, I encountered Satan echoing somehow from inside. He was full of insults and threatening. Immediately, Jesus Christ also descended inside the house and He got on commanding Satan off. He was shouting to him; *"You Satan, see that open door, get out so that it be closed. I say do it, get out!"*Although the devil was radical, hesitant and loud but still, he saw the door. After that, I perceived of it completely closed and noted that both Jesus and Satan were on the outside. Immediately there came three entities, masquerading as angels of light. 2 Corinthians 10:13-15.The word of God says this; *"Beloved, do not believe every spirit but test the spirit to see whether they are of God"* - 1 John 4:1 As those three beings came, they said; *"Alright, Kokote, we have brought to you all that you've asked from God".* I asked them; *"what will you tell me about Jesus Christ, who was crucified, died and resurrected?' what of His bruises that He suffered for me and my wife and the whole world that we may be healed?"* Immediately, they were confused and started hurling insults at me and murmuring; *"Kokote is a real fool. We have come from God to give him his gifts and now, see what he is telling us".* Immediately as I recognized that they were angels of darkness, I rebuked them in the mighty name of Jesus Christ of Nazareth and they were off. From the outside, I could perceive of myself somewhere audibly preaching, praying and binding demonic spirits.

The devil was telling Jesus; ***"See him, now, he can't be able to do God's calling. Please let me get him, I have a special offer for him."*** Jesus answered him; ***"Oh Satan leave him alone, God Himself will enable him".*** The devil retorted; ***"And why can't I be left to get his wife?"*** Jesus Christ shouted to him, ***"Satan, leave them alone. It's God Himself who is going to enable them".*** The whole of that debate was very clear, but my wife could not perceive of what was going on.

CHAPTER 12

SALVATION.

One day, I was sharing the word of God with a friend of mine. We were talking about salvation and he told me that there was no need for salvation. He added that whenever he prays, he was sure that his prayers went to God. ***"So what is the need of being born again?"*** He boasted. First of all, I showed him the word of God in the book of 1Corinthians 1:18- ***"He is the source of your life in Christ Jesus, whom God made, our wisdom, our righteousness and sanctification and redemption. Therefore as it is written, 'let him who boasts, boast of the Lord."***

In John 14:6"Jesus said to him; ***'I am the way, the truth and the eternal life. No one comes to the father except by me."***

Definitely, no one will ever prosper if he actually locks Jesus Christ in a box and directly goes to worship the father. If you worship God that way, it's as if you worship Him while you are blindfolded.

As the ribbon is put off your eyes, you will just be astonished to see that the one you'd been worshipping is the devil. He will devise many avenues for you to worship God, but alas! It's the devil - Ezekiel 28:1-10.

2Corinthians 4:3-6 *"And even if our gospel is veiled, it is veiled only to those who are perishing. In their case the god of this world has blinded the minds of the unbelievers, to keep them from seeing the light of the gospel of the glory of Christ, who is the likeness of God."*2Corinthians 5: 17; *"Therefore if anyone is in Christ, he is a new creation; the old has passed away, behold, the new has come."*

2 Corinthians 6: 1-2; *"At the acceptable time I have listened to you, and helped you on the day of salvation. Behold, now is the acceptable time; behold, now is the day of salvation."*

Hebrews 2: 1-3, *"How shall we escape if we neglect such a great salvation?"* In the book of Romans 10: 8-11 the word of God says, *"Because, if you confess with your lips that Jesus is Lord and believe in your heart that God raised him from the dead, you will be saved."* It also says, *"No one who believes in Him will be put to shame."*

Dear reader, if you have not yet let Jesus Christ come into your heart and save you from the judgment of God to come, you just say this prayer of repentance right now where ever you are.

"My dear Lord Jesus Christ, I am a sinner and I know this, forgive me of all the sins and transgressions that I have ever committed. Erase my name from the book of death and write it in the book of life; sanctify me by your precious blood. I am now born again in the mighty name of Jesus." Amen!

If you have prayed this prayer of repentance, you are now born again in Jesus Christ. Still, it's most advisable for you to get a pastor or a mature born again person to lead you in this prayer of faith.

The probability for you to stay upright and sober in your salvation is higher than when you do it alone. It's also good for you to pray to God to make you gain access into a church which is spiritually awake rather than in a spiritually dead church. In a lukewarm church, you also grow lukewarm which might send you onto the backsliding bench. God is faithful.

If you pray to Him about where you should be worshipping, He will just do it for you. Here I am going to illustrate three case `study of three women. One happened in the spiritual realm while the other two happened in the physical realm. Two of the women each came to me for prayers/deliverance. One was a Christian by faith whom I call (Susan) not her real name. The other one was a Muslim whom I call (Fatma) not her real name.

a) Susan came to me while I was in my sister's house. I usually paid her a visit from time to time. that woman actually waited at a time when my sister had gone to the market-of course they were neighbors. I later learned that she was a true sorceress.

She came directly, knocked at the door and as I opened it and welcomed her, she entered and sat directly upon the floor while I sat on a chair. Of course she felt comfortable on the floor instead of sitting on a chair.

"Are you okay there on the floor or maybe, do I give you a chair?" I asked her. *"No, I am okay."* She answered and went on to ask me this question; *"I always hear you testifying about Jesus. Have you ever seen Him?"*

I answered her; *"Not yet, I just do it by faith as the word of God proclaims"*

Hebrews 10:38-39 says, *"But my righteous one shall live by faith, and if he shrinks back, my soul has no pleasure in him."* Ref Hebrews 11:6.

She then said that she usually saw Him and asked Him a lot of questions. She also said that there is a very big city- the devil's city right in the heart of the sea. She noted that inside the devil's house, there is some decoration of 500 shillings tiles on its walls. On its floor there are some decorations of 200 shillings tiles. She said that the devil has some two horns and a tail. He also used to demonstrate his musical prowess to them. When he closed one nostril and blows the remaining one, only gospel music came out. When he did the vice versa, its only worldly music that came out. She used to ask him; *"why do you say that you are god and that you should be worshipped yet you have some horns and a tail?"* *"Well"* he answered, *"These are just for decoration, but I am still god and every person shall have to be worshipping me."* Ezekiel 28:1-20. About seeing the genuine Jesus Christ or the true holy angels of God, the Bible warns 1 John4:1, *"Beloved, do not believe every spirit but test the spirits to see whether they are of God..."*

I told the young woman that the devil is a great liar. He is a thief, a killer and a destroyer. John 10:10.

"The devil has taken you captive and so, you need to have some prayers for your deliverance." I told her. *"Yes"* she accepted. *"That's why I have come to you. I have noted that you are more mature than your sister and mind you, I was recruited by a woman from Nairobi by the name (Pauline) not her real name."* Towards the end of her story, my sister came back and as she listened, she asked her, *"Mama Selinah, you have gone that very far and we don't know yet you are our neighbor."*

I told her that I would lead her in the prayer of repentance and then pray for her. She accepted but said, *"Just before you pray for me, I shall have to tell you this; most pastors and some other people that had prayed for me earlier, I felt that they didn't have enough power to pray and heal me. As they prayed, I noted that their tongues protruded as long as a knife and I could measure their power and noted that they didn't have enough of it to heal me."*

I told her; *"Well, that is your own perception. No one can really heal you except only Jesus Christ of Nazareth. He died, resurrected and was bruised that we may be healed. You used to put your faith upon those people but now do it the other way round. Put your faith upon Jesus Christ and you shall be alright."* Romans 10:11. I prayed for her and later, the next day, she came and told me; *"Last night, as I prayed, I heard some demonic voices that said, "even if you chase us away, we will go to Nigeria."*

I told her to keep on praying that those dark forces should never find an easy and clean house to live in her.

 b) I had not known Fatma at first but about her demonic oppressions news, I was informed by my sister in law- wife to my brother. She told me that Fatma was her friend and used to dodge her teaching lessons and stayed at home instead due to her demonic oppression. Sometimes she was sent to hospital but she escaped. She had fallen into that trap-the race -1 Kings 19:1-3. In the said day, I was in my brother's house just watching T.V. That woman came in, wearing a black veil and carrying a baby. As she was welcomed, she just sat on a couch and watched T.V with us. I didn't know whether that young woman was the one that her story was told to me. As we watched T.V, I testified about Jesus to her and the rest and at once she asked me; *"can you pray for me?"* That young woman was frustrations all over her face and also greatly alarmed.. I asked her; *"why do you feel that you need some prayers?""I feel that I am fixed by the devil and I don't know what to do. Every night there are some men-not my husband who come to my home and sleep with me and I am tired of this. I don't really feel that I have the power to resist them. Pray for me if you can."* "Well", I said, *"I can for surely pray for you, but your eyes and mind, fix them upon Jesus. He is the one to heal you."*

I first of all prayed for her and made her to enter into the covenant of salvation with Jesus Christ. Thereafter, I just prayed a prayer of deliverance upon her life.

Immediately after the prayers, she turned out to be a total different person. She became exceedingly happy and wore a peaceful smiling face. She said, *"I need that you also pray for my kids. They have also fallen into a demonic trap."* She had two kids and while she carried one with her, the other one was at home. I told her; *"Go get him here."*

I had never yet prayed for children, but the word of God requires that one should act in total faith. Hebrews 10:38-39. I prayed for them and she was totally happy. As our Lord Jesus was letting her jump and frolick in the garden/paradise of total happiness, she told me, *"Wait, can you do me one more favour?"* I said; *"Yes, what is it?" "My husband, Pray for him also that he may be born again."*

I told her to go in peace, that her husband would follow suit and be born again as she would keep holding onto the salvation. After all that, my brother and his wife told me; *"do you know that you have made a grave mistake? You have prayed for a soldier's wife, you know, it's really unthinkable."*

I told them that I could not resist the fear that was in her face. That young woman was severely harassed by the devil. But then, there is a superpower more than all superpowers in heaven above and down on earth. God's superpower that operates under the name of Jesus Christ the best forever. Ephesians 1:19-23; *"And what is the exceeding greatness of his power towards us who believe, according to the working of His mighty power which he performed in Christ, when he raised him from the dead and set him at his own right hand in the heavenly places. Far above all principalities, power, might, dominion and every name that is named, not only in this age, but also in that which is to come. And has put all things under His feet, and gave Him to be the head over all things to the church which is His body, the fullness of Him that fills all in all."* Have a safe journey in this great salvation that the Lord has given us. Hebrews 2:1-3

c) The third woman's case happened in the spiritual realm. I perceived of her to be an Indian, a sorceress and a high priestess of an unknown satanic sect. It happened while I worked as a night security officer around Mama Ngina area-Mombasa. I had already prayed and had gone on browsing through the internet. In the mid of what I was doing, I realized that I was surrounded by a commotion from the dark world. I could perceive of a fleet of cars, and the owners, most of them-Indians. They had come for me as they were complaining that I was troubling their dark operations in that area.

That sorceress was in one of those storey buildings around that place. She seemed to be the head of the whole of that evil congregation. There were other people around her and she seemed to be confused. She kept on quarrelling in a language I could not perceive. Immediately, I rebuked those ones on the ground with their vehicles in the mighty name of Jesus Christ of Nazareth and at once, they were off. However, of that woman, as hard as I rebuked her, she was still confused and quarrelling. I then said; *"Jesus Christ my Lord and master, the word of God Isaiah 53:5 says that you were bruised such that we are healed. My dear Lord Jesus, reveal yourself to that woman and her companions as when you were bruised and crucified upon the cross."*

Dramatically and at once, I perceived of that woman plus her companions worshipping in front of Jesus.

Jesus Christ had revealed Himself to them and that woman was actually worshipping and saying, *"Hail, the blood of Jesus, Jesus we need your grace. Forgive us of our sins for we repent before you oh Lord." Later on, in the following days, it was that woman entity plus a man entity-probably the high priest and a few others praying. Every morning at around 2am and beyond, they were really worshipping and calling upon the blood of Jesus. About mentioning the blood of Jesus, it's never a small issue. It's almost a taboo for those dark forces to mention that statement "the blood of Jesus"*

All the others were almost always confused as they saw their leaders forsaking their evil stronghold and parading behind Jesus Christ of Nazareth. Thus, the kingdom of Satan was divided against itself. Mark 3:25-26, *"and if a house is divided against itself, that house will not be able to stand. And if Satan has risen up against himself and is divided, he cannot stand, but is coming to an end."*

Ref. Isaiah 14.

CHAPTER 13

<u>GOD'S ARMOUR AND THE BELIEVER'S AUTHORITY</u>

As one reads the word of God, he can easily note that the weapons of God are quite plenty. It's like when the word of God in Matthew 11:28 says, *"come to me all of you who labour and are heavily laden and I will put you to rest."* I had seen this working practically several times as a weapon in my life. I had a pastor pray with me the prayer of repentance and so I am a born again Christian. I used to go to church but I was still bound by the spirit of drunkenness and cigarette smoking. I knew that no one would break that bondage away from me except the one who uttered those words Matthew 11:28. I used to tell Jesus;

"Jesus Christ my good Lord and Saviour, I know that it's you only that has and gives out eternal life. You died, resurrected and was bruised so that we may be healed. You redeem your people by sanctifying them by your precious blood. Look at me dear Lord, smoking this cigarette and its half way now. Do you love me this way? It's truly a bondage and a burden upon my shoulders. Dear Jesus, I come before your

throne. Break these bondages of cigarette smoking and drunkenness off me."

If it were not for our Lord Jesus Christ, I would still be a slave to those evil bondages. Whenever you are grieving in anything, just cry out to Him for help. Whatever you utter towards Him, it has to come out from deeply out of your heart John 4:22-24. He died and resurrected and now He is alive. Just talk to Him and He is there to give you help. I had come to know also that whenever you use one weapon always, it will sometimes not work. God would be expecting you to use various weapons as found in the bible. In the book of Ephesians 6:10-12 the word of God says; ***"finally my brethren, be strong in the Lord and in the power of His might; put on the whole armour of God that ye may be able to stand against the wiles of the devil. For we wrestle not against flesh and blood, but against principalities, against powers, against the rulers of darkness of this world, against spiritual wickedness in high places."*** You can also read 2Corinthians 10:3-16.

In Ephesians 10:17, the word of God says; ***"And take the helmet of salvation and the sword of the spirit, which is the word of God."*** I had used this sword of the spirit in many occasions. This is just done in faith. Whenever I had come across an evil congregation pertaining those workers of iniquity, in the spiritual realm, I first of all ask Jesus Christ, my master to put upon me the whole armor of God.

And I said; *"Hey, you workers of iniquity, here I hold the sword of the spirit in my right hand. Now, get lost in the mighty name of Jesus."* As clearly as in the day, they just shoot their eyes at me and alas! They see me holding in my hand a strange and an amazing sword. They might also start teasing me about this sword and they said; *"It's not a big issue; of course he doesn't know how to use it."* They might jump to attack me as I also jumped to attack them and I said; *"In the mighty name of Jesus, I use this mighty sword against your heads, hands and legs."* I would just repeat those words for some few minutes until everything comes to a standstill. They would later say; *"He has killed some people. He is ruthless. Why does he like oppression?"* others might cry;

"Father, Kokote is killing us." They are also confused easily and you can command them to get to specific destinations especially if they are demonic spirits. In the book of Jeremiah 23:29 the word of God says, *"Is not my word like fire? Said the Lord and like a hammer that breaks out the rock in pieces?"* Psalms 29:4-5

says; *"The voice of the Lord is full of majesty. The voice of the Lord breaks the cedars; the Lord breaks the cedars of Lebanon."* I have used these and so many other weapons within the word of God and the outcome was awesome. Spiritual warfare for everyone born again is just a normal thing as the word of God in Matthew 10:34-39 says; *"Do not think that I have come to bring peace on earth; I have not come to bring piece, but a sword. For I have come to set a man against his father and a daughter against his father, and a daughter in law against her mother, and a daughter in law against her mother in law, and a man's foes will be those of his own household."*

In Joel 3:9-10; the word of God says; *"Proclaim this among the nations. Prepare for war, stir up the mighty men. Let all the men of war draw near, let them come up. Beat your plough shares into swords, and your pruning hooks into spears;let the weak say, I am a warrior."*

In Jeremiah 48:10 the word of God says, *"Cursed be he that doeth the work of the Lord deceitfully, and cursed be he that keeps back his sword from bloodshed."* Dear readers; there is totally no exception in this. The devil feels that he has authority over all people and that is why he does not shy to go and contest for the spiritually upright people like in the book of Jude verse 9-

"But when the arch angel Michael, contending with the devil, disputed about the body of Moses, he did not presume to pronounce a reviling judgement upon him, but said, 'The Lord rebuke you"

Zechariah 3:1-2; *"Then He showed me Joshua the high priest standing before the angel of the Lord and Satan standing at his right hand to accuse him. And the Lord said to Satan, 'The Lord who has chosen Jerusalem rebukes you! Is not this a brand plucked from the fire?"* As I discerned all of that spiritually, I have come to know that most people, especially the ones that are not covered by the precious blood of Jesus and divinely protected by God are in a dire danger. In most of the cases the devil kills them temporarily as he takes them captive latter to be offered as human sacrifice. My friend! You are in a dire danger if you are not yet born again.

If only God gives you an opportunity to have a glimpse of the devil and what he is doing in the darkness against you, then you wouldn't be grazing in his grass field. To be born again, sometimes one has to use some force to come out of the devil's hoax, Matthew 11:12. No one can be able to fight this spiritual warfare while he is not born again and not living in an upright life pertaining Godliness.

Our Lord Jesus Christ has already given us authority and He said: Matthew 28:18-20, **"All authority in heaven and on earth has been given to me. Go therefore and make disciples of all nations, baptizing them in the name of the Father and of the Son and of the Holy Spirit, teaching them to observe all that I have commanded you, and I am with you always, to the end of the ages."** Read also Matthew 10:1, this authority goes hand in hand with faith and prayers combined with fasting.

Mark 9:28-29 **"And when he had entered the house his disciples asked him privately, why could we not cast it out?** and he said to them, **'This kind cannot be driven out by anything but prayer."** You can also read Matthew 17:19-21. Our Lord Jesus Christ has already given us authority. Every person in this world is bound to exercise this authority. This calls for every person to get born again, choose to live a life pertaining Godliness, get hold of the authority and start this spiritual journey.

Most people think that they are safe doing whatever they

are doing in this world. They feel that God has given them jobs, wives, husbands and different vocations.

No one in this world can be able to do anything except that God gives them the power, strength and the authority to do it. The fact is that some people are and will soon be compromising their authority to the devil. The truth in all of this is that no one is needed to go to Jesus and start begging for the authority. You just do what He says and tell Him, ***"Jesus, thank you for giving me this authority."*** When you proclaim to have this authority, you can be sure that those entities sitting in the kingdom of darkness will surely look at you and say, ***"Alas! He has that authority"*** if you tell God; ***"My Lord give me this authority."*** Then the devil looks on and say; ***"See he has no authority and so he is begging God to give him. I will go and give him my authority."*** The devil seeks to change everyone's Godly given authority with his. Revelation 13:2, my dear friend, you better start using this Godly given authority, or else the devil will soon change it with his. Very soon, many people will forgo their Godly given authority and do Satan's biding instead. Make haste and choose life John 10:10.

Dear reader, you can actually read this for reference- Judges 16:15-21, and revelations 13:1. It's utterly dangerous for one to just compromise his Godly given authority to the devil. This is actually shown in Judges 16:15-21 when Samson compromised his Godly given authority via his treacherous wife.

About forgiveness of sins and transgression, this falls between God Himself and the man of God. Every person has his own account to give before God.

The devil has got some machinery to scan people and know whether they are truly born again or not. He also has his own dictionary containing the explanation of three groups of people.

i. The first one comprises of the truly born again Christians. These have accepted Jesus Christ in their lives. Their sins are truly forgiven and Jesus Christ has sanctified them by His holy blood. God's glory is upon them and so, they are divinely protected. The devil knows that these are not his, but he wedges war against them to win them over to his side. Those that just carry their bibles, attend church but have nothing to do with salvation and Godliness, the devil knows that they are hypocrites and so he says; ***"All the hypocrites are mine."***

ii. The second group pertains of the devil's agents.

These are the ones that are directly answerable before him. They actually have meetings and fellowship with him directly and he says, ***"These are mine."*** They comprise of witchdoctors, sorcerers, most religious sect members, members in secret societies and many more people whom are pursuing different types of vocations within the devil's umbrella. These may comprise some of scientists, students, engineers and much more. All of them, automatically, the devil says; "***They are mine.***"

iii. The last group comprises of all of those people who live just an Ignorant/passive life. These either feel that there is no God, have another god altogether or else they don't feel that salvation is a must. They worship the devil absent minded and the devil says, "***All of them are mine.***"

Deuteronomy 30:19, the word of God says, "***I have set before you this day life and destruction.***" It's God Himself whom has offered people those two choices. You choose as you wish and He is never a dictator. The devil is a dictator but God just looks on as you choose prerogativelly heading towards that fatal trap. It's advisable that all people should make a choice that when they die, they should die in the Lord Jesus Christ. Revelation 14:13; "***And I heard a voice from heaven saying, 'write this;***

blessed are the dead who die in the Lord henceforth, blessed indeed, says the Spirit, that they may rest from their labor, for their deeds follow them". Ref - Psalms 116:15, I bid all the readers of this book a safe journey as you choose to come onto God's side and fight the good fight - 1Timothy 6:12.

Before I close this chapter, I will write a little bit about what happens to a person who has got bondages and who also fasts and prays about their calamities. Maybe you might not have known that you have bondages but immediately you start praying, you might end up getting confused. God is not the author of confusion 1Corinthians 14:33 and so you must resist it and command it off to hell in Jesus' Mighty name.

When a person is living with some bondages and he is feeling that he is living a comfortable life, that's just not right. This is just because those evil spirits that are in line with those bondages are just sticking there and comfortable about it because there is no one whom has blown the whistle on them. Whenever an upright born again Christian prays, the devil is easily confused, challenged and ready to run. As he is confused, he also appears to be much confident, violent and proud. However, he has already raised his trousers ready to run.

This happens as in the case of Goliath versus David and the children of Israel, 1 Samuel 17:1. Goliath depicts the devil when he is confused. Mind you if you don't have a stable faith-a coward, you might start the race at once. Here, before you start running just for nothing, this is what God is telling you; Jeremiah 1:17-19,

"But you, gird up your loins; arise, and say to them everything that I command you. Do not be dismayed by them, lest I dismay you before them and I, behold, I make you this day a fortified city, an iron pillar, and a bronze wall, against the kings of Judah, its princes, its priests and the people of the land. They will fight against you, but they shall not prevail against you, for I am with you, says the Lord to deliver you."

Whenever you pray, bind evil spirits, nullify them, destroy them and cast them to hell, it's advisable that you tarry for a little while as you do it. One should tarry in this until they at least feel a wave of peace. There was some time I used to pray and cast off evil spirits to hell but alas! They used to stick on to the top of the mouth of hell - Isaiah 5:14. As I became tired and summed up my prayers, that evil spirits/stronghold started flying back towards my direction. Immediately they touched down on earth, they started their evil operations at once.

Almost all good things people do on earth; an account is reserved in heaven Matt 6:19-21. When people give offerings, tithe in the house of God, when they also give to the poor, preach, testify or pray, an account reflects in heaven. There were times whereby I could have prayed and latter on, the same day, the second or the third day, I could see that line of prayers unveiling in the spiritual realm- one word after the other. Things like when I prayed that Jesus Christ comes down and take over the war. I would have arrested the devil and his evil battalion and also asked God to let down His angels to carry my wife and I up in their hands such that we might not stumble on those dark forces. These and more things I could have asked God for in Jesus' mighty name and they would unfold one word after the other as I perceived of it happen in the spiritual realm. I could then perceive of my wife and I held high and above all the powers of darkness. I could also perceive of demonic spirits groping in the darkness as they could not see their way through while we were held off their path by God- Psalms 91:11-12.

CHAPTER 14

<u>CAN A BORN AGAIN CHRISTIAN BE DEMON POSSESSED?</u>

There is one thing that I have noted under the sun. I have come across some certain films whereby the commando would pick one soldier from his battalion whom he says is guilty. He takes him plus all the others to a place in the forest and orders the guilty one to start running. He then commands the rest, armed, to go after him and shoot to kill, like in the film-DEADLY PRAY. This is what the devil likes doing to people and it doesn't matter whether someone is born again or not. He shoots a threat at you and if you turn to run, then you are possessed. As you keep on running, he is right there after you and he is serious. The devil is never a joker as most of we Christians seem to think. The threat might be anything let say a sickness, a serious case, and some rumors about war or anything else. Instead of staying put and seek the Lord, you start running. You go to a native doctor or start running from one place to another like in Isaiah 36:12, the word of God says *"But the Rabshakeh said, has my master sent me to you, and not to the men sitting on the wall, who are doomed with you to eat their own dung and drink their own urine?"* Thanks for the servant of God; King Hezekiah who offered prayers and supplications to God and God's intervention was swift. In the book of 1Samuel 17:1- we read about the Israelites and Goliath. That's how the devil acts. He is actually a terrorist and the father of it all terrorism. Thanks for the Israelites whom retreated a little bit, just around the same place and took positions. Most of them could have been praying fervently. God had chosen David the son of Jesse to stand in the gap and cast off that fearsome giant with all his evil wishes. In the book of Jeremiah 1:27, God told Jeremiah the servant of God;

"Do not be dismayed by them, lest I dismay you before them." In my case when everything started, I set my feet ready to start running wondering whether God was there to protect me. God gave me the same warning and I stood my ground.

The word of God put it very clearly that for the born again Christians, it's only the ones sinning and transgressing that are demonically possessed, Ecclesiastes 10:8, ***"He who digs a pit will fall into it, and a serpent will bite him who breaks through a wall."*** Whenever a person is born again, God puts a hedge around him. That person is divinely protected by God. If that person chooses to do the things that the word of God says don't, he is then demonically possessed. One can read the word of God in Numbers 21:4-9 and 1Corinthians 10:1-5 for reference. In Ezekiel 18:4, the word of God says; ***"Behold, all souls are mine; the soul of the father as well as the soul of the son is mine; the soul that sins shall die."*** One day, the Lord had enabled me to have a friend near me whom we were working together. I had noted that he was newly born again, straight from devil worship and was not yet delivered. He told me that he was born again but I could clearly see that he had frustrations. During that time, I didn't know how to help such a person who says that he is already a born again Christian but not yet delivered. He used to tell me that he saw things before they happen and so on.

One day he had come to our house and as we both went out, he told me that he could see some fire actually descending from the sky and entering my room.

He added that that fire was following us from behind as we walked on. He also said; ***"Look, I can see some fire, golden in colour surrounding you. Do you also see it?"*** - Zechariah 2:5;I told him that he might be seeing it but I wasn't seeing any of it. I didn't marvel so much in this because every born again and upright person is supposed to have that hedge- a Godly protection. Seeing into the spiritual realm happens to the servants of God but devil agents also see into the things of God. They have their own gadgets to enable them identify the people whom are truly born again and upright so that they can wedge war against them. Those wise men who came to see Jesus when He was born were stargazers from the east. They saw the star and knew that one who would be king was born. They knew it and so they went to Jerusalem to look for Him so that they could worship Him. They went there while the church was dormant. It was prophesied in the word of God but the church was in deep sleep. They didn't know whether it had already happened.

God divinely protects his people as one day happened to me. I was asleep and as I woke up, I noted that there were evil spirits confused and running away and they said; ***"How does Kokote worship God? There are three angels surrounding him. This shows that he is a mature born again Christian. These angels also appear as soldiers."*** This is a favor that every born again Christian has from God Isaiah 49:16.

But wait until when one goes onto the other direction, stealing, taking alcohol, committing adultery, going to witchdoctors and so on-doing the things that God says don't. It is here that you see someone demonically possessed or actually start living with bondages (curses).Pertaining the things of God, ignorance has got its pay and revelers have got their path and gate set already. In Matthew 7:13, the word of God says; ***"Enter by the narrow gate, for wide is the gate and broad is the way that leads to destruction and the way that many go in by it.".***

In the book of Isaiah 35:8-10, God has put a high way for the righteous. Dear reader, you might think that you are just alright living without bondages or demonic oppression, but wait; do you neglect this great salvation? Hebrews 2:3.

ABOUT THE AUTHOR

Hamena .J. Kokote is in his forties, and lives in Kenya. Conquering The Powers of Darkness is the title of his first book. He is already working out another book with a different title which will soon be in the market. He is a vessel of honour in God's own hand. He has also graduated as a motor vehicle technician.